Tracy & Wayne Gill
45 Kendale Road

CW00894188

ENGLISH

CurriculumBan

KEY STAGE ONE
SCOTTISH LEVELS A-B

SPELLING AND PHONICS

LIZ LAYCOCK AND ANNE WASHTELL

Published by Scholastic Ltd,
Villiers House,
Clarendon Avenue,
Leamington Spa,
Warwickshire CV32 5PR
Text © 1996 Liz Laycock and Anne Washtell
© 1996 Scholastic Ltd
234567890 6789012345

AUTHORS
LIZ LAYCOCK AND ANNE WASHTELL

EDITOR
KATE BANHAM

ASSISTANT EDITOR
CLARE GALLAHER

SERIES DESIGNER
LYNNE JOESBURY

DESIGNER
CLARE BREWER

ILLUSTRATIONS
MICK REID

COVER ILLUSTRATION
GAY STURROCK

INFORMATION TECHNOLOGY CONSULTANT
MARTIN BLOWS

SCOTTISH 5–14 LINKS
MARGARET SCOTT

Designed using Aldus Pagemaker
Printed in Great Britain by Ebenezer Baylis & Son,
Worcester

British Library Cataloguing-in-Publication Data
A catalogue record for this book is available from the
British Library.

ISBN 0-590-53391-6

The rights of Liz Laycock and Anne Washtell to be identified as the Authors of this work have been asserted by them in accordance with the Copyright, Designs and Patents Act 1988.

All rights reserved. This book is sold subject to the condition that it shall not, by way of trade or otherwise, be lent, hired out or otherwise circulated without the publisher's prior consent in any form of binding or cover other than that in which it is published and without a similar condition, including this condition, being imposed upon the subsequent purchaser.

No part of this publication may be reproduced, stored in a retrieval system, or transmitted, in any form or by any means, electronic, mechanical, photocopying, recording or otherwise, without the prior permission of the publisher. This book remains copyright, although permission is granted to copy pages 110 to 157 for classroom distribution and use only in the school which has purchased the book.

Contents

Introduction

Scholastic Curriculum Bank is a series for all primary teachers, providing an essential planning tool for devising comprehensive schemes of work as well as an easily accessible and varied bank of practical, classroom-tested activities with photocopiable resources.

Designed to help planning for and implementation of progression, differentiation and assessment, *Scholastic Curriculum Bank* offers a structured range of stimulating activities with clearly-stated learning objectives that reflect the programmes of study, and detailed lesson plans that allow busy teachers to put ideas into practice with the minimum amount of preparation time. The photocopiable sheets that accompany many of the activities provide ways of integrating purposeful application of knowledge and skills, differentiation, assessment and record-keeping.

Opportunities for assessment are highlighted within the activities where appropriate. Ways of using information technology for different purposes and in different contexts, as a tool for communicating and handling information and as a means of investigating, are integrated into the activities where appropriate, and more explicit guidance is provided at the end of the book.

The series covers all the primary curriculum subjects, with separate books for Key Stages 1 and 2 or Scottish Levels A–B and C–E. It can be used as a flexible resource with any scheme, to fulfil National Curriculum and Scottish 5–14 requirements and to provide children with a variety of different learning experiences that will lead to effective acquisition of skills and knowledge.

SCHOLASTIC CURRICULUM BANK ENGLISH

The *Scholastic Curriculum Bank English* books enable teachers to plan comprehensive and structured coverage of the primary English curriculum, and enable pupils to develop the required skills, knowledge and understanding through activities.

Each book covers one key stage. There are four books for Key Stage 1/Scottish levels A–B and four for Key Stage 2/Scottish levels C–E. These books reflect the English programme of study, so that there are titles on Reading, Writing, Speaking and listening and Spelling and phonics.

Bank of activities

This book provides a bank of activities that provide opportunities to talk about similarities and differences in words, as well as opportunities to play with words and take part in word games. Such contexts capitalise on children's innate interest in language and provide valuable learning areas.

Lesson plans

Detailed lesson plans, under clear headings, are given for each activity and provide material for immediate implementation in the classroom. The structure for each activity is as follows:

Activity title box

The information contained in the box at the beginning of each activity outlines the following key aspects:

▲ *Activity title and learning objective.* For each activity a clearly stated learning objective is given in bold italics. These learning objectives break down aspects of the programmes

of study into manageable, hierarchical teaching and learning chunks, and their purpose is to aid planning for progression. These objectives can easily be referenced to the National Curriculum and Scottish 5–14 requirements by using the overview grids at the end of this chapter (pages 9 to 12).

▲ *Class organisation/Likely duration.* Icons †† and ◷ signpost the suggested group sizes for each activity and the approximate amount of time required to complete it.

Previous skills/knowledge needed

Information is given here when it is necessary for the children to have acquired specific knowledge or skills prior to carrying out the activity.

Key background information

The information in this section outlines the areas of study covered by each activity and gives a general background to the particular topic or theme, outlining the basic skills that will be developed and the ways in which the activity will address children's learning.

Preparation

Advice is given for those occasions where it is necessary for the teacher to prime the pupils for the activity or to prepare materials, or to set up a display or activity ahead of time.

Resources needed

All of the materials needed to carry out the activity are listed, so that the pupils or the teacher can gather them together easily before the beginning of the teaching session.

What to do

Easy-to-follow, step-by-step instructions are given for carrying out the activity, including (where appropriate) suggested questions for the teacher to ask the pupils to help instigate discussion and stimulate investigation.

Suggestion(s) for extension/support

Ideas are given for ways of providing easy differentiation where activities lend themselves to this purpose. In all cases, suggestions are provided as to ways in which each activity can be modified for less able or extended for more able children.

Assessment opportunities

Where appropriate, opportunities for ongoing teacher assessment of the children's work during or after a specific activity are highlighted.

Opportunities for IT

Where opportunities for IT present themselves, these are briefly outlined with reference to particularly suitable types of program. The chart on page 158 presents specific areas of IT covered in the activities, together with more detailed

support on how to apply particular types of program. Selected lesson plans serve as models for other activities by providing more comprehensive guidance on the application of IT, and these are indicated by the bold page numbers on the grid and the ⌨ icon at the start of an activity.

Display ideas
Where they are relevant and innovative, display ideas are incorporated into activity plans and illustrated with examples.

Aspects of the English PoS covered
Inevitably, as all areas of English are interrelated, activities will cover aspects of the programmes of study in other areas of the English curriculum. These links are highlighted under this heading.

Reference to photocopiable sheets
Where activities include photocopiable activity sheets, small reproductions of these are included in the lesson plans together with guidance notes for their use and, where appropriate, suggested answers.

Assessment
Children's development as spellers will take place over time. For this reason we have included photocopiable record sheets for different aspects of phonics and spelling knowledge, rather than suggesting one-off summative assessments. Every activity provides an opportunity for teachers to observe and record aspects of individual children's developing knowledge, skill and understanding of words, letters, alphabetical order, spelling patterns, use of dictionaries, and so on. It is

suggested that a copy of each record sheet is made for each child and that a file is created for these. At the end of a school year, if they are completed regularly, they will give a great deal of detailed information about each child's spelling ability. Some photocopiable sheets (for example, 'Introducing consonants and vowels') could be used as diagnostic, baseline assessments of children's current knowledge, and these too, should be added to the child's file. As Margaret Peters (1985) says, 'Conventional spelling tests tell us too little about a child's spelling. Since spelling is an individual, all-or-nothing skill, we should find out more about the strategy a child uses in spelling.' Diagnostic activities will contribute to teachers' understanding of a child's spelling and enable plans to be made to offer appropriate support and teaching. Assessment activities are indicated by the ✍ icon.

Photocopiable activity sheet
Many of the activities are accompanied by photocopiable activity sheets. For some activities there may be more than one version to provide differentiation by task. Other sheets may be more open-ended to provide differentiation by outcome. The photocopiable activity sheets provide purposeful activities that are ideal for assessment and can be kept as records in pupils' portfolios of work.

Cross-curricular links
Cross-curricular links are identified on a simple grid which cross-references the particular areas of study in English to the programmes of study for other subjects in the curriculum, and where appropriate provides suggestions for activities (see page 160).

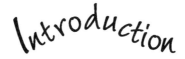

SPELLING AND PHONICS

The starting point for children's learning about letters and the alphabet is generally their own name because this has become familiar to them long before they arrive in school. The written form of a name is often the child's first recognisable string of letters and this becomes the resource to generate further writing. We believe that the name activities will be particularly beneficial to all children, however limited their experience.

Knowledge of the alphabet is clearly fundamental both to successful learning of sound/symbol relationships and in spelling development. This book, therefore, places a strong emphasis on acquiring this knowledge in a variety of ways. We recognise that some teachers will want to teach the letter names of the alphabet as a universal language with which to discuss the alphabet. The advantage in this is that the terms remain constant when discussing a specific letter, whereas the sound may not, for example in 'acorn' and 'Alice'. Equally, other teachers will wish to use the initial sound of the word under discussion. For this reason, in some of our activities, for example the 'I Spy' activities, we have provided for this variation of approach. It is likely that most teachers will choose to vary their approach in different situations and will make their own decisions in this matter.

The development of 'phonological awareness' has recently been shown to be a necessary skill which affects children's progress in learning to read. When they come to literacy, children have a great deal of implicit knowledge about their language, but they are not generally able to identify and analyse this knowledge.

Other research has demonstrated that children's progress in learning to read is better when they show sensitivity to rhyme and alliteration before they begin to learn to read. It has been shown that children's awareness of the onset/rime distinction* is very important in their phonological development. What this research seems to point to is that teachers need to develop children's awareness of rhyme and alliteration, and sensitivity to onset and rime, before they focus too heavily on the fine distinction of grapheme/phoneme correspondence.

With all this in mind, we have provided activities with a strong emphasis on rhyme and alliteration and activities on letter strings which develop children's existing awareness of onset and rime. The 1995 National Curriculum Programme of Study for Reading at KS1 highlights these Key Skills:

(2b) 'Phonic knowledge, focusing on the relationship between print symbols and sound patterns. Opportunities should be given for:
▲ recognising alliteration, sound patterns and rhyme, and relating these to patterns in letters;
▲ considering syllables in longer words...'

The second of the National Curriculum Key Skills for Reading at KS1 is:

(2b) 'Graphic knowledge, focusing on what can be learned about word meanings and parts of words from consistent letter patterns, including:
▲ ...spelling patterns in verb endings;
▲ relationships between root words and derivatives, eg. help, helpful;
▲ prefixes and suffixes.'
This is echoed in the Key Skills for Writing at KS1:

(2d) 'In spelling, pupils should be taught to:
▲ write each letter of the alphabet;
▲ use their knowledge of sound–symbol relationships and phonological patterns;
▲ recognise and use simple spelling patterns;
▲ write common letter strings within familiar and common words;
▲ spell commonly occurring simple words;
▲ spell words with common prefixes and suffixes.'

The activities provided here are all informed by these requirements. Children's early attempts at spelling words they wish to write draw heavily on their phonic knowledge and even, at times, on their knowledge of letter names. While children's attempts to spell independently through 'inventing' spellings should never be undervalued or discouraged, teachers will need to intervene to help focus attention on the visual factors and clues, which is the ultimate aim in becoming a good speller.

---

* Onset and rime: 'The onset is the opening consonant or consonant cluster if the syllable does begin in such a way and the rime consists of the vowel sound and any following consonants; every syllable therefore has a rime though not every one has an onset. So, "s" is the onset and "and" is the rime of "sand"; and "str" the onset and "ing" the rime of "string".' Bryant (1993)

Our emphasis in the activities designed to develop spelling is strongly visual; activities which are derived from Pelmanism, Kim's Game or Happy Families require children to look closely at words in order to visualise and remember them. In their own writing, especially at the editing stage, children should be given words when they ask for them but they should not copy them down letter by letter. The earliest possible development of the 'look–cover–write–check' routine for learning words will help children to focus on the appearance of words, rather than relying solely on the sounds.

In providing these activities we recognise that the development of phonic knowledge and spelling can be supported through a range of well- structured and progressive activities and we have often attempted to outline a series of activities which build upon each other to develop the children's knowledge. Sometimes materials are made by the children, in the course of one activity, which can then be used to develop further skills in a subsequent activity. We would emphasise, however, that the use of the suggested activities should be a part of a wider perspective, where children's current knowledge and understanding of phonics is acknowledged and supported in the context of their reading, when they read aloud from a piece of continuous prose. Similarly, the appropriateness of provision of spelling activities for the child at any particular stage can only be judged from analysis of the child's current thinking and understanding in the context of their individual writing. Most of the activities suggested would be appropriate for only some of the class at any particular time.

A FRAMEWORK FOR DEVELOPING A SCHOOL POLICY

For any area of the curriculum, it is essential to have a clear, cohesive policy for teaching throughout the school. HMI and OFSTED point continually to the correlation between clear, understood, agreed approaches, consistently implemented, and children's success and high levels of achievement. The evidence suggests that this is certainly true for reading; the particular approach adopted seems to be less significant than the consistency with which it is applied.

This must surely also be true for teaching about phonics and spelling. Nothing is more confusing for children than to have this year's teacher insist upon different things from last year's teacher. We have suggested, in this book, that there are two essential strands in Key Stage 1 in teaching about phonics and developing phonemic awareness – these are work with the alphabet and work on rhyme and alliteration. For spelling, we have suggested that, although children must be encouraged to experiment with their own invented spellings, drawing on their knowledge of sound–symbol relationships, they must also be encouraged to develop their visual awareness of words. These principles underpin suggestions made here for considering a school policy.

Resources in Key Stage 1

If work on the alphabet, rhyme and alliteration is to be consistent a range of resources will be required:

▲ children's name cards, in as many contexts as possible;

▲ alphabets, in the form of published friezes and charts, as well as class- and teacher-made charts and friezes, sets of alphabet cards and puzzles;

▲ a range of different kinds of alphabet books;

▲ wherever possible, 'big books' of the alphabet for shared reading, which is a good context for teaching about letters and words;

▲ nursery rhyme books of many kinds, along with other rhymes and poems;

▲ rhymes of all kinds made into large display cards for shared reading;

▲ a range of children's books, with patterned, rhyming, alliterative language;

▲ computer software (for example, *Animated Alphabet*).

For work on spelling strategies, resources should include:

▲ reference charts, showing common, regularly-used words (days of the week, number words, class names);

▲ regularly-changed charts of collections of words (word banks) relating to current themes, topics, interests (for example, spellings of different animals, minibeasts, homes);

▲ picture dictionaries, simple conventional dictionaries, spelling activities on computers;

▲ reminders (posters) of what to do to find a word and how to set about memorising words (look–cover–write–check).

9

Introduction

Agreed approaches

Issues for consideration, leading to agreed approaches:

▲ how much time will be given to work on children's alphabetic knowledge (this may be different in nursery or reception classes and Year 2);

▲ how progression will be ensured, so that children will not repeat the same things year after year;

▲ will letter names and/or sounds be used in alphabet work;

▲ whether children are to be introduced to both upper and lower case written forms of letters;

▲ whether all teachers understand the recognised stages in children's development as spellers (if not, should some staff development time be allocated to this);

▲ how spelling teaching is to be integrated into teaching writing, at what stage in the writing process is spelling, rather than composing, to be emphasised;

▲ how children will be given the confidence to experiment with spelling;

▲ expectations for spelling in children's writing; the strategies children will be taught when composing (having a go, circling/underlining words they are unsure of, strategies for finding words, use of word-books);

▲ what strategies children will be taught for learning new words (look–cover–write–check for words they are told; personal challenges/word lists);

▲ what connections will be made with handwriting policy to foster links with spelling;

▲ how to respond to children's writing/spelling;

▲ how children will be taught about checking their spelling (following first writing and revision);

▲ how to help children develop awareness of visual patterns in words ('looking with intent', word games, collecting word families, looking for letter strings);

▲ how to assess and record progress in both phonic knowledge and spelling;

▲ how to inform parents about the school's approach and the reasons for it.

These are all big questions, but agreed approaches to all these matters will need to be arrived at, if a cohesive policy is to be implemented. It is not the purpose of this book to prescribe approaches, although the activities suggested will reflect the author's views. Each school must decide on the approach which best meets their children's needs and teachers will need to liaise closely to evaluate the effectiveness of the approaches used.

Further reading

Adams, M.J. (1990) *Beginning to Read: Thinking and Learning about Print*, Heinemann

Bissex, G. (1980) *GNYS AT WRK: A child learns to write and read*, Harvard University Press

Bradley, L. and Bryant, P. (1983) 'Categorising sounds and learning to read: a causal connection' in *Nature* No. 301

Bradley, L. and Bryant, P. (1985) *Children's Reading Problems*, Blackwell

Bryant, P. (1983) 'Phonological aspects of learning to read' in Beard, R. (1993) *Teaching Literacy: Balancing Perspectives*, Hodder & Stoughton

Bryant, P. et al. (1989) 'Nursery Rhymes, Phonological Skills and Reading' in *Journal of Child Language*, Vol. 16

Bryant, P. and Goswami, U. (1990) *Phonological Skills and Learning to Read*, Lawrence Erlbaum Associates

Carter, R. (ed.) (1990) *Knowledge about Language and the Curriculum*, Hodder & Stoughton

Clay, M. (1975) *What Did I Write?*, Heinemann

Clay, M. (1993) *Reading Recovery: a Guidebook for Teachers in Training*, Heinemann

Cox, B. (1991) *Cox on Cox: an English Curriculum for the 1990s*, Hodder & Stoughton

Cripps, C. (1978) *Catchwords Ideas for Teaching Spelling*, Harcout, Brace, Jovanovitch

Cripps, C. and Cox, R. (1989) *Joining the ABC*, Cambridge

Crystal, D. (1987) *The Cambridge Encyclopaedia of Language*, Cambridge University Press

DFE (1995) *English in the National Curriculum*, HMSO

Ferreiro, E. and Teberosky, A. (1982) *Literacy Before Schooling*, Heinemann

Gentry, J.R. (1981) 'Learning to Spell Developmentally' in *Reading Teacher* Vol. 34 (4)

Gentry, J.R. (1987) *SPEL... is a four letter word*, Scholastic

Newman, J. (1987) *The Craft of Children's Writing*, Scholastic

National Writing Project (1989a) *Becoming a writer*, NFER Nelson

National Writing Project (1989b) *Responding to and assessing writing*, NFER Nelson

National Writing Project (1989c) *Writing and Micros*, NFER Nelson

Peters, M. (1990) *Spelling: Caught or Taught? – A New Look*, Routledge

Peters, M. (1993) 'The Teaching of Spelling' in Beard, R. (ed.) *Teaching Literacy Balancing Perspectives*, Hodder & Stoughton

Peters, M. and Smith, B. (1993) *Spelling in Context*, NFER Nelson

Redfern, A. (1993) *Teacher Timesavers: Spelling and Language Skills*, Scholastic

Redfern, A. (1993) *Practical Ways to Teach Spelling*, Reading and Language Information Centre, University of Reading

Smith, B. (1994) *Teaching Spelling* Minibook 5, UKRA

Smith, F. (1986) *What's the Use of the Alphabet?* Reading and Language Information Centre, University of Reading, in conjunction with Abel Press, Victoria B.C.

Torbe, M. (1991) *Teaching Spelling* (revised edition), Ward Lock

Vellender (Washtell), A. (1989) 'Teacher inquiry in the classroom: what's in a name? Literacy Events in an Infant Classroom' in *Language Arts*, Vol. 66 (5)

Overview grid

Learning objective	PoS/AO	Content	Type of activity	Page
The alphabet				
Developing knowledge of alphabet. Identifying initial letter sounds.	Reading: 2a, 2b. Sp. & List.: 1. *Reading for info.: Level A. Spelling: Level A.*	Making up alliterative descriptions to go with own name. Illustrating these to go in class alphabet book.	Whole class, talking about alphabet, sounds in children's names. Compiling book.	16
Developing knowledge of alphabet. Focus on upper case forms.	Reading: 2a. Writing: 2a. *Reading: Level A.*	Children making upper-case letters with their own bodies. These are photographed for display.	Whole or half class bodily creating letter shapes. Compiling class display/ book of photographs.	17
Developing knowledge of initial letter sounds. Introducing alphabetical order.	Reading: 2a, 2b. Writing: 2d. *Reading: Level A. Spelling: Level A.*	Children writing own names and illustrating for class ABC book.	Whole class discussion on initial letters. Writing own names. Introducing alphabetical order.	19
Making connections between sounds of initial letters (phonemes) and objects beginning with particular sound.	Reading: 2b. Sp. & List.: 1c, 3b. *Reading: Level A.*	'I Spy' using classroom objects. Focusing on initial (and sometimes final) letter sounds.	Whole class talking about initial letter sounds. Assessment of children's knowledge of phonemes.	20
Practising 'I Spy' using characters from story book; initial sounds.	Reading: 1, 2b. Sp. & List.: 1c, 3b. *Reading: Level A. Writing: Level A.*	Reading aloud *Each Peach, Pear, Plum*. Teacher scribing children's 'I Spys' to make large book illustrated by children.	Whole class listening to book. Individuals making illustrated contribution. Re-reading completed book with whole class.	21
Developing alphabetic knowledge: focus on initial letter-names and sounds.	Reading: 2b. Sp. & List.: 1c, 3b. *Reading for info.: Level A.*	Children using name cards, naming initial letters and sounds. Recognition of written forms of names.	Whole class or small group. Speaking and listening to focus on alphabet knowledge.	23
Developing alphabet knowledge. Phonemic discrimination using children's names.	Reading: 2b. *Listening for info.: Level A.*	Playing 'I Spy' using names of children in the room.	Whole class or large/small group, listening to and identifying initial phonemes.	25
Developing knowledge of letter names/sounds. Recognising written letter forms.	Reading: 2b. Sp. & List.: 1c. *Reading: Level A.*	Naming objects, linking initial sound to the written letter.	Small group, talking about and naming letters. 'Reading' individual letters.	26
Identifying and sorting names according to initial letter.	Reading: 2b. Sp. & List.: 1c, 2a. *Reading: Level A.*	Playing 'Happy Families' using sets of names with same initial letter.	Small group, talking about letters, naming letters.	28
Developing familiarity with letters of the alphabet and their sequence.	Writing: 2d. Reading: 2a. *Reading: Level A. Functional Writing: Level A.*	Sound/symbol correspondence. Reciting alphabet. Making labelled food item for each letter. Displaying in order.	Whole class discussion, then small groups or individuals making and labelling own named items to contribute to display.	30
Developing knowledge from previous activity (letters and sequence).	Reading: 2a. *Reading: Level A.*	Identifying alphabetical order and position of letters.	Whole class discussion of sequence of letters of the alphabet.	33
Identifying initial and final sounds/ letters in words. Single consonants/ initial consonant digraphs and blends.	Reading: 2a. *Reading: Level A.*	'I Spy': initial letter/sound = final letter/sound of previous object. Then play written version.	Small/large group. Oral identification of initial/final sounds. Writing and reading of chosen words.	34

11

SPELLING AND PHONICS KS1

Overview grid

Learning objective	PoS/AO	Content	Type of activity	Page
Developing recognition of initial consonant sounds/blends/digraphs.	Reading: 2b. Sp. & List.: 2a, 3b. *Reading: Level A.*	Playing game to create word chain; final sound/letter to match initial sound/letter of next word.	Small group/pairs reading words and identifying initial sounds/blends/digraphs.	36
Writing the alphabet, using children's forenames.	Writing: 2d. Sp. & List.: 1c. Reading: 2b. *Functional Writing: Level A.*	Compiling class list in alphabetical order. Making own class lists for use in future activities.	Whole class discussion of alphabetical order. Individual writing of alphabetical class list.	38
Memorising sequence of alphabet. Linking individual letters with initial sounds of words.	Reading: 2a. Sp. & List.: 2b, 3b. *Reading: Level A.*	Playing alphabetical shopping list game; one object for each letter.	Whole class or group; oral recall of list, reinforcing alphabetical order.	39
Writing each letter of the alphabet. Reinforcing alphabetical order.	Writing: 2d. *Writing: Level A.*	Making individual alphabet books with one item for each letter.	Whole class; recitation of alphabet, then individual writing of alphabet in order.	41
Developing phonological awareness; knowledge of alphabet sequence and initial sounds and letter names.	Reading: 2a. Writing: 2d. *Reading: Level A.*	Children sorting themselves into alphabetical order. Remembering order.	Whole class, sorting selves into alphabetical order. Discussion of position in alphabet.	44
Sorting names according to initial letter.	*Reading: 2b Reading Level A.*	Sorting books into order according to author's name.	Whole class or group, then individuals. Sorting.	46
Rhyme and alliteration				
Listening to and identifying rhyming sounds.	Reading: 1a, 2a, 2b. Sp. & List.: 1a. *Listen in order to respond to texts: Level A.*	Reciting nursery rhymes. Identifying rhymes in well-known nursery rhymes.	Group or whole class, speaking and listening.	50
Connecting sound patterns in rhymes and letters in print.	*Reading: 2b. Sp. & List.: 1a, 2b. Writing: 2d. Reading: Level A. Writing: Level A.*	Reciting nursery rhymes, picking out rhyming pairs of words; writing rhymes.	Whole class listening for rhymes, then pair or small group work, reading and identifying written rhymes.	52
Developing awareness of initial consonant phonemes. Recognising letter patterns of words.	*Reading: 2b. Sp. & List.: 1c, 2a. Writing: 2d. Reading: Level A. Listening: Level A.*	Using a selection of rhyming words to identify rhyme families.	Small group, speaking and listening; hearing rhymes and identifying written rhymes.	54
Identifying differences in sound patterns and rhyme. Locating these in written forms.	Reading: 2d. Sp. & List.: 3. Writing: 2d. *Reading: Level A. Listening: Level A.*	Oral identification of words which do not rhyme in a set of words. Card game: 'Odd One Out' sorting according to rhyme.	Small group listening for rhymes. Written words to read and sort.	56
Helping children to hear differences in sound patterns and rhyme. Linking these to patterns of letters.	Reading: 2b. Writing: 2d. *Reading: Level A.*	Using terminology 'rhyme'/'pattern'. Identifying odd one out in a set of words.	Small group. Individuals read out words and collect sets of same family.	59
Applying oral knowledge of rhyme and written forms of rhyming words. Introduction of opposites.	Reading: 2b. Writing: 2d. *Writing: Level A.*	Reading nursery rhyme, spotting rhymes. Making up poem with rhyming pairs.	Whole class or group. Discussion then shared writing composing rhyme.	61

SPELLING
PHONICS

Overview grid

Learning objective	PoS/AO	Content	Type of activity	Page
Developing alphabetic knowledge and sensitivity to alliteration.	Reading: 2b. Writing: 2d. *Reading: Level A. Writing: Level A.*	Selection of alliterative word to go with own name. Write and illustrate these for class book.	Whole class introduction, then individual writing activity. Reading completed book.	63
Experiencing and heightening awareness of alliteration.	Sp. & List.: 2b. Reading: 2b. *Reading: Level A. Listening: Level A.*	Reciting and creating tongue-twisters with initial single consonants/ consonant digraphs.	Group activity, reading aloud. Children listening for alliteration.	65
Developing knowledge of alliteration.	Reading: 2b. Sp. & List.: 1a, 3b. *Listening: Level A. Writing: Level A.*	Reading aloud tongue-twisters. Composing variation of a well-known one.	Group activity, discussion of tongue-twisters, alliterative sounds identified. Shared writing composition of further tongue-twister.	66
Consolidating children's knowledge of alliteration. Focusing on written patterns in alliterative sentences.	Reading: 2b. Sp. & List.: 1a, 3b. *Writing: 2d. Writing: Level A.*	Listening to and composing alliterative sentences, editing and spelling alliterative words.	Whole class discussion of alliterative sentences. Pairs of children writing own alliterative sentences.	69
Syllables				
Providing experience of hearing rhythm. Recognising similarities and differences in rhythms.	Reading: 2b. Sp. & List.: 1a, 2b. *Reading: Level A.*	Reciting nursery rhymes, clapping syllable rhythms (mono/polysyllabic).	Whole class or group listening, reciting and counting syllables.	72
Identifying syllables in words.	Reading: 2b. Sp. & List.: 1a, 2b. *Listening: Level A.*	Listening to rhythms of rhymes; clapping rhythms of own names; counting number of syllables.	Whole class or group listening and repeating rhythms/syllable patterns of words.	73
Recognising monosyllabic/ polysyllabic words. Introducing term 'syllable'.	Reading: 2b. Sp. & List.: 1a. Writing: 2d, 3b. *Listening: Level A.*	Children clapping name rhythms. Sorting names according to number of syllables and making a chart; making name cards showing number of syllables.	Whole class or group. Listening for number of syllables: sorting and writing name cards.	75
Practising identification of monosyllabic/polysyllabic words.	Reading: 2b. Sp. & List.: 1a, 2b. Writing: 2a. *Reading: Level A.*	Card games using children's names of different syllable lengths. Sorting into sets.	Small group, playing game with teacher.	77
Working with polysyllabic words. Introducing compound words.	Reading: 2b. Writing: 2d. *Reading: Level A. Writing: Level A.*	Creating compound words. Labelling and illustrating them	Whole class or small group orally listening for and joining 2 words to create compound word.	79
Combining monosyllabic words to form new two-syllable words.	Reading: 2b. Writing: 2d. *Reading: Level A. Writing: Level A.*	Creating two-syllable words. Card game, matching 2 halves of compound words.	Small group, talking about combining words; labelling, playing card game.	81
Analysing sounds in polysyllabic words.	Reading: 2b. *Reading: Level A.*	Clapping syllables in children's names, then in names of living creatures. Marking and cutting into syllables.	Small group, listening and discussing what they notice. Clapping rhythms and segmenting words into syllables.	83

13

SPELLING AND PHONICS KS1

Learning objective	PoS/AO	Content	Type of activity	Page
Analysing polysyllabic words. Making (??) sounds in syllables to graphic form.	Reading: 2b. *Reading: Level A.* *Spelling: Level A.*	Revision of syllables. Game rebuilding three-syllable words. Definition of syllable.	Pairs or small group discussion of syllables in order.	86
Consolidating and making explicit children's knowledge of syllables.	Reading: 2b. *Reading: Level A.*	Card game; sorting words into sets of appropriate number of syllables.	Small groups. Discussion and use of terminology including consonant/vowel.	88
Drawing on children's knowledge of syllables. Compose 'haiku'.	Reading: 2b. Sp. & List.: 2b. Writing: 1c. *Imaginative* *Writing: Level B.*	Discussion of haiku form/ syllabic pattern and of Japanese context.	Whole class introduction. Shared writing of poem. Individual writing using worksheets to brainstorm/ draft.	89
Graphic knowledge				
Introducing terms 'consonant' and 'vowel'. Consolidating alphabetic knowledge.	Reading: 2a. Writing: 2d. *Reading: Level A.*	Alphabet knowledge; number of letters, letter names, distinguishing consonants/vowels. Identifying vowels/ consonants in own names.	Class or small group, singing/reciting alphabet. Identification of vowels and consonants.	94
Using terms 'vowel' and 'consonant'.	Reading: 2a. *Reading: Level A.*	Recitation of alphabet; using charts and alphabet cards to identify vowels and consonants. Sorting own name cards according to initial vowels/consonants.	Small group(s) talking about words and their structure. Reading names and classifying according to initial letters.	96
Consolidating knowledge of initial consonant blends.	Writing: 2d. Reading: 2b. *Reading: Level A.* *Spelling: Level A.*	Playing 'Happy Families'- type game, matching sets of words with same initial consonant blend. Learning to spell these words.	Small group. Recognising and memorising initial consonant blends with 's'. Spelling test on words used.	97
Familiarising children with common letter strings in words. Usual identification of letter-strings/words in longer words.	Writing: 2d. Reading: 2b. *Spelling: Level A.*	Game using cards with common letter strings. Aim: to collect sets and learn the spelling pattern.	Small group. Reading words and collecting sets with the same letter patterns.	99
Identifying common letter strings/ words in longer words.	Writing: 2d. Reading: 2b. *Spelling: Level A.*	Finding small words, using the letters in the same order, in longer words.	Individual/small group word search: locating words/ familiar letter strings.	100
Familiarising children with sets of words having the same letter patterns.	Writing: 2d. Reading: 2b. *Spelling: Level A.*	Timed writing of known words with particular letter strings in them.	Pairs: visual recall of common letter strings.	101
Identifying common letter strings and patterns.	Writing: 2d. Reading: 2b. *Spelling: Level A.*	Pelmanism: collecting pairs of cards with the same letter string.	Small group. Reading words/learning words with consistent letter patterns.	103
To introduce suffixes as tense markers.	Writing: 2d. Reading: 2b. *Spelling: Level A.*	Card game adding suffixes to regular and irregular verbs.	Small group. Playing Pelmanism trying to match a verb card with a suffix.	104
Introducing the term 'prefix' and looking at prefixes 'un-' and 'dis-'.	Writing: 2d. Reading: 2b. *Spelling: Level B.*	Card game adding negative prefixes to roots to make words of opposite meaning.	Pairs of children: recording words created on work sheet.	106

SPELLING AND PHONICS KS1

The alphabet

The letters of the alphabet have been described as 'the soldiers of literacy' and our written language system is completely dependent on these 'soldiers'. The alphabet performs many complex roles. Identifying these roles takes time and to understand them fully takes even longer.

The first thing that children need to realise is that the written symbols that they see on paper represent the words that they hear and speak. They need to understand that there is a direct link between the smallest unit of sound in spoken words (phonemes) and the smallest unit of sound in written words (the grapheme or single letter). Alphabet knowledge, both spoken and written, is essential for this.

Children need to learn the letter names of the alphabet in order to equip themselves with a 'metalanguage', or a way of speaking about letters that can be applied universally and will enable them to talk about and analyse any word. For example, using the short 'a' sound as in 'Alison' may be confusing for children if it is also used to discuss the long 'a' in 'Amy'. It is essential, though, in the first stages of reading that children also learn to identify the sounds that letters make, paying particular attention to the initial and final sounds of words.

Children's names are deliberately used as a resource for alphabet work. Names are frequently the first words that children can spell consistently, with the initial letter often being the first grapheme that children pay attention to. This awareness of the initial letter of their name often marks a significant early link with other words.

15

NAME ALPHABET

To develop knowledge of the alphabet. To identify initial letter sounds.

†† *Large group or whole class, then individuals.*

🕘 *20–30 minutes with the whole group; 20–30 minutes to complete, either in the same session or the next day.*

Previous skills/knowledge needed
Children should be familiar with the written form of their own names. Experience of sorting name cards in various ways, including alphabetically, would be helpful.

Key background information
This activity entails making an alphabet using the name of each child with an accompanying descriptive word. It is intended to focus on the connection between the written letter form and the sound this makes as the initial letter of the child's name. The ability to perceive letter sounds is an essential prerequisite to making sense of phonic instruction; the use of another word with the same initial sound helps to make this 'sameness' explicit to the children in a humorous and playful context.

Preparation
Make a list of all the names of the children in the class. These could be written out on large sheets of paper, with spaces for the addition of the 'other words', or the children's name cards could be attached (with Blu-Tack) to an easel or board.

Resources needed
Large sheets of paper and felt-tipped pens or writing board and chalk or pens, a selection of published books with alliterative titles – eg. *Noisy Nora* by Rosemary Wells (1978, Armada), *Sleepy Sammy* by Rose Impey (1994, Orchard) – writing materials, art materials.

What to do
Ask the children to sit where they can all see the names display. Read through the names, perhaps asking individuals to identify their own. Ask the children to point out those names that begin with the same letter/sound.

Explain that you are going to make a class alphabet, using everyone's name with a describing word. It is probable that not all 26 letters of the alphabet will be represented, but begin with those that are. Show the children some books which use names in this way, for example *Noisy Nora*. Talk about words which describe people and give a few examples, perhaps using your own name, for example Clever Claire or Brave Bill. Let them each have a go with their own name first and then allow others to make suggestions. Once a suitable descriptive word has been chosen, write that word alongside the appropriate name.

Continue working in this way as a group as long as the children are involved and interested. Then allow the children to go off to continue alone. Those who have chosen the words for their own names can begin designing an illustration. Those who have still to choose a word should work with a partner or in a small group to support one another and, once these have chosen, they should tell the teacher, who then adds it to the large sheet. Then they, too, can draw their illustrations.

As the pictures are completed, the teacher should write the text clearly on to paper which is then attached to the picture. The finished names and pictures should be displayed in alphabetical order, leaving gaps for any missing letters. This will help the children to identify where they need to find

other names in a later session. If the display is to be fairly permanent, it is best if the captions are written by an adult so that the writing is very clear and can be read easily by the children.

Suggestion(s) for extension
The gaps in the name alphabet could be identified and listed as a small group activity. The group can then visit other classes to find suitable names, or make a list of family members, and choose appropriate descriptive words for these. Individual children can each choose one to work on until the alphabet is complete.

Suggestion(s) for support
Those children who have difficulty thinking of an appropriate descriptive word could work in pairs to pool ideas.

SPELLING AND PHONICS KS1

Assessment opportunities

Make a note of children's individual knowledge of letter sounds and their awareness of 'same sound' words. Note particularly those who do not seem able to hear sounds so that further activities can be planned for them. Note, too, any who seem to know a range, or even all, the letters in the alphabet. Different work on letter sounds will be needed for them.

Listen out for comments or questions which reveal the child's current understanding/awareness. Make a note of these.

Opportunities for IT

Children could use a simple word processing package to type and print out their names and captions. This would give young children an early opportunity to enter and print work using the computer which is not too keyboard intensive. It would also be an ideal way of introducing children to some simple keyboard skills. The teacher could set up a large font style or even a border around the page so that children had only to enter their name and caption word and then print their work.

Where children are confused by the use of upper case letters on the computer keyboard small sticky labels with lower case can be stuck to the keys. Alternatively, a concept keyboard can be linked to the computer with an overlay showing just lower case letters. These can be made larger and so are ideal for very young children. Some mouse driven software such as My World enables children to select and drag the letters they want on to the writing area of the screen.

Display ideas

The completed name alphabet should be mounted (with the children's help) on to larger sheets of paper or card on to which each letter, in upper and lower case forms, are written. This should be displayed at the children's eye-level so that it can be used as a point of reference for alphabetical order and information about individual letters.

Aspects of the English PoS covered

Reading – 2a, b.

BODY ALPHABET

To make an alphabet focusing on upper case letter forms.

†† *Half class.*

🕐 *2 or 3 sessions of 30–40 minutes.*

Previous skills/knowledge needed

This activity can be done with groups of children who have varying knowledge of the letters of the alphabet. Those who have little knowledge will gain experience of some letter shapes and names; others will learn a few more whilst those who know many can experiment with making their shapes with their own bodies.

Key background information

This activity is particularly useful for working with a group with a wide range of knowledge and ability because children can draw on whatever knowledge they have and because the physical element of the activity allows all to participate. There is evidence that the physical manipulation of materials,

drawing on several senses, helps children to learn letter shapes. In this activity children will soon realise that some letters can be formed with their own bodies, whilst others will require collaboration in twos, threes and fours. They will also notice that the capital letters, because they have more straight lines, are easier to make than lower case letters.

Preparation

A large space will be needed for the children to move around in and to allow them to work in groups – the school hall is ideal, if that can be arranged. Some letter shapes will need the children to work physically closely, so it is a good idea to remove shoes and socks.

Resources needed

An alphabet frieze or poster which shows upper and lower case letter forms and which is easily portable; a camera suitable for taking indoor photographs, loaded with a 36 exposure film, for the teacher's use in the final session.

What to do

After taking the children into the movement space, gather them together where they can all see the alphabet poster or frieze. Ask them to look at the letter shapes and notice the differences between upper and lower case forms. Explain that you will be asking them to try to make the shapes of the letters using their bodies and ask them to choose which one they would like to start with. Explain that they can work alone or with partner(s). It does not matter if several children wish to do the same letter to begin with.

Allow them to move away and begin experimenting. When you see a successful attempt at a particular letter, stop the children and ask those children to demonstrate their letter

to the others who should then try to guess the letter. Do this several times, selecting some solo letters and some where the children have collaborated. Discuss with the children whether they have made capital letters or lower case letters. Most will be capitals so this point should be emphasised and the children invited to consider why. Make a note of which children succeeded with which letter, for future reference.

In the next session remind the children of their previous success and work more systematically through the alphabet so that all the children attempt most letters. By the end of this session it may be possible to photograph each letter/ group. If the children need further work leave the photography until the third session.

When all the letters have been created ask the children to watch each individual or group make their letter while you take a photograph of it, making sure that you take the picture from the angle which will give the correct orientation when it is printed! Get the photographs processed as soon as possible so that any unsuccessful ones can be re-done before the children forget what they did.

Suggestion(s) for extension

For children who seem to know most or all of the letter forms, provide booklets for them to make their own alphabet books, with or without captions giving an object beginning with each letter, as appropriate.

Suggestion(s) for support

Provide opportunities for those children who are still unsure of the letter shapes to make them in Plasticine, with construction materials, to cut them out of paper or to paint them.

Assessment opportunities

Make notes about individual children's letter knowledge throughout the activity.

18

At the end of the session complete a checklist of which letters can be:
▲ recognised;
▲ named;
▲ formed in Plasticine;
▲ written.

Display ideas
As soon as the photographs are complete display the whole set alongside the poster or frieze where they can all be seen and discussed.

Aspects of the English PoS covered
Reading – 2a.

ABC

To develop alphabetic knowledge. To identify initial letter sounds.

†† *Whole class, then individuals.*

🕐 *15–20 minute introduction with the whole class; 20–30 minutes to complete individually; 10 minutes with the whole class to read the completed book.*

Previous skills/knowledge needed
Children all know their first names and some may know the first letter of their names. They should be familiar with ABC books, such as *Lucy and Tom's A.B.C.* by Shirley Hughes (1984, Gollancz) and should have been encouraged to link the first letter of their names to the appropriate page. They will have to have talked about letter order, whose name comes first, and so on.

Key background information
Children's own names are generally the first words in which they begin to recognise letters. The initial letter is often regarded as 'their' letter. This activity draws on the children's existing knowledge and begins to develop a fuller knowledge of the alphabet and alphabetical order.

Preparation
Ensure that all children are familiar with the idea of an ABC book. Prepare a large ABC book using sheets of A2 paper folded in half to create 26 A3-sized pages. These can either be sewn along the fold or stapled with a long-arm stapler. Label each page alphabetically with an upper case letter. Prepare A5 paper for the children to write their names on and/or illustrate with a picture of themselves (these will be fixed in the book later). Each child's piece of paper should have their individual initial letter printed on it. Display a list of the children's names either on a flip chart or on the chalkboard to refer to with children when necessary. Prepare name cards for those who may need them.

Resources needed
Large blank ABC book, one sheet of lettered paper (A5) for each child, name cards, class list (prepared as above), pencils, illustration materials, adhesive.

What to do
Explain to the class that you want them to help you make a Class name book and that you will be putting all their names in alphabetical order. Remind the children of previous experiences with ABC. Show the children the prepared ABC book. Take each letter in turn and ask the children to think whose name starts with which letter. If children ascribe a name to the incorrect letter, for example 'Philip' to the 'F' page, encourage discussion about alternatives. Draw attention to any pages that will have more than one name on them. Similarly, draw attention to pages, for example 'X', that may have no entries.

Then ask the children to find a piece of paper with their letter on it and to write their name and draw a picture of themselves. As children complete the task ask them to find the correct page in the ABC book and to stick their work in.

Once the book is finished read it through with the children.

Suggestion(s) for extension
On pages where two or more names appear, encourage the children to look at the similarities and differences in the sounds of the names; for example, Anita and Amarjit both start with the 'a' sound, but although 'Paul' and 'Philip' both start with the letter 'P' they have different sounds at the start of their names. Encourage the children to think of other names that they could use to fill up the pages that have no entries. The task could be made more complex by asking the children to make an ABC book organised by surnames. Alternatively, an alliterative name book would provide a further challenge (see activity on page 63).

Suggestion(s) for support

For a very inexperienced class the whole activity could be carried out through 'shared writing', that is with the teacher scribing straight into the prepared large ABC book as the children talk and interact with her. The children could then draw pictures of themselves on paper labelled with their initial letter which would then be pasted into the book.

In a class where individual children are experiencing difficulty ask them to write the letters of their names that they do know and scribe the remainder for them or write the complete name out for them whilst commenting on the sounds and formation of the letters. These children can then draw themselves. Some children may feel more confident if they can trace over letters or copy their name card.

Assessment opportunities

Notice who can/cannot link the first letter of their name with the ABC. Listen for comments on pages where more than one name occurs about similarities and differences in the sounds of the names. Children may make rhyming connections between names and other words with which they are familiar, for example 'Lee' sounds like 'see'. Encourage children to talk about the length of their name and draw attention to the last sound in their names. On subsequent re-readings observe how they go about locating their page in the book and comments they make about their names, for example: 'There's "ice" in "Alice".' Note which children can/cannot write their names unaided.

Opportunities for IT

Children could use a simple art package to create their ABC class names book. This would involve using both text and pictures on the same drawing page. Children could type in their name and then use the art package to draw a picture of themselves. They could be introduced to some of the simple commands of the art package; drawing lines, changing

colours and changing the size and shape of the brush. When finished these could be printed out and used to make a class book.

Alternatively children could write their name into the ABC book using a word processor into style set up in advance by the teacher and print it out. They could then draw a picture of themselves. This could be an extension of 'Name alphabet' with children working more independently at the computer.

Display ideas

The completed ABC book should be placed in the book corner and used for regular 'shared book experience' sessions. An alternative to the children drawing themselves would be to take a set of photographs and use these to illustrate the book. The book can also be used by the children to find their friends' names when they want to spell these.

Aspects of the English PoS covered

Reading – 2a.

 **'I SPY'**

To help children understand the connection between the sound of a letter and a particular object that is represented by that sound.

†† *Small or large group activity.*

⏱ *15 minutes.*

Previous skills/knowledge needed

Some knowledge of initial/final letters would be helpful. However, this game is well suited to complete beginners.

Key background information

Children need to be able to hear the sounds which make up words (phonemes) before they can begin to make the connection between the sounds of words and the printed symbols. Many children need considerable practice in this activity and the focus on the initial sound of a word is the easiest place to start.

Resources needed

None needed for basic game. Photocopiable page 110 for assessment.

What to do

Explain to the group that you will be playing 'I Spy' with them. Check whether they are familiar with the key rules, that is, that the objects being 'spied' *must* be visible to everyone *within* the classroom and that, when taking their turn, the children should provide a clue as to the name of the object by naming the first sound. If the children are unfamiliar with the game, it may be necessary to remind them about the turn-taking rules.

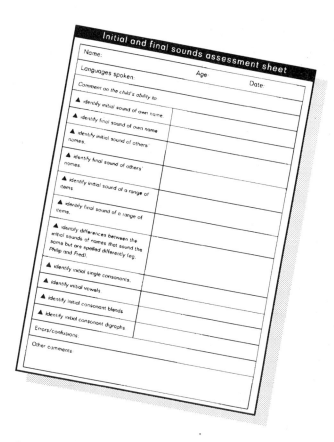

Start the game off in the usual way by saying, 'I spy with my little eye, something beginning with... (the letter sound).' The first child to provide the correct response then takes his/her turn. The game continues until all the children have participated. As the children play, the teacher should note, on photocopiable page 110 'Initial and final sounds assessment sheet', the extent to which individuals are able to identify sounds in different positions in words.

Suggestion(s) for extension
Children who demonstrate confidence in identifying words by initial sound could be further challenged by being asked to identify the final sound of each word that they correctly 'spy'. In addition, they could be asked how many letters they think are in the word and finally asked to spell the word aloud.

The game can be played in the same way using the name of the letter instead of the sound.

Suggestion(s) for support
Children who find the conventional form of 'I Spy' too challenging can be supported by working with a partner with whom they can confer before attempting to offer solutions. Working with a partner will also support these children when taking their turn to select an object and successfully decide on its initial sound. Those children who find it difficult to establish the link between the letter sound and the object may also benefit from being given additional clues about the physical properties of the object, for example: 'I spy with my little eye, something beginning with "c". It's round, has numbers on it and it hangs on the wall...' (Clock.)

Assessment opportunities
Through what they say, children will reveal how far they are establishing links between letter names or sounds and objects. It is important not only to note correct responses but also to record information about errors, such as confusion between 'k' and 'c'. More experienced children will demonstrate knowledge of initial and final letters and sounds and in some cases their ability to spell words.

Aspects of the English PoS covered
Speaking and listening – 1c; 3b.
Reading – 2b.

Reference to the photocopiable sheet
The 'Initial and final sounds assessment sheet' can be used over time to record children's growing ability to identify letters and sounds at the beginning and end of words. The sheet could be used at several points in the year to indicate development.

'EACH PEACH' I SPY BOOK

To introduce children to the skill of identifying an object by the initial letter of its name.

†† *Small or large group activity.*

🕐 *Initial activity – 30 minutes; follow-up sessions – 30 minutes.*

Previous skills/knowledge needed
This activity is well suited to beginners or children who find regular 'I Spy' games too complex. The children should, at least, have been introduced to the game of 'I Spy'.

Key background information
The routine of looking, identifying and naming a character or object is essential knowledge needed by young children before they can begin to ascribe letters or sounds to words they know.

The alphabet

Preparation

Make a Big Book for the children's work, using sheets of plain or coloured A2 paper, folded in half to make A3-size pages. The centre fold should be either stapled or stitched. Write the title 'Each Peach I Spy Book' on the front cover.

Resources needed

Each Peach Pear Plum by Janet and Allan Ahlberg (1989, Penguin) (preferably large format); flip chart and pens, ready-made blank Big Book for children's work, drawing paper, coloured pencils or crayons, pencils.

What to do

Explain to the group that you are going to read *Each Peach Pear Plum* to them and that you are going to ask them to help you play 'I Spy' as you read the story. Ascertain how much the children know about how to play 'I Spy' and then read the story to them. The story is likely to be highly interactive, with the children eager to spot the characters and where they are hiding in the illustrations as they go along.

Having read the story through once, go through it again, this time focusing on the characters and where they are hiding. Ask the children to help you remember who is hiding in the story by asking, 'Who can you spy in the story? I'll start with "I Spy Tom Thumb".' Write 'I spy Tom Thumb' on the flip chart and ask the children 'Who else can you spy in the story?' As they identify the characters frame their ideas with 'I spy... (name of character), and write each one on the flip chart. The children may want to add other items, eg. 'I spy lots of trees,' or 'I spy the bears' chairs.' Accept all their ideas and add them to the list.

To conclude the oral form of the activity, when everyone has had a turn, ask each child to recall his/her idea. Start off by saying, 'Each peach pear plum, I spy Tom Thumb.' Ask each child to follow your pattern, 'Each peach pear plum, I spy...' Alternatively, the child's name can be substituted for the personal pronoun 'I', for example 'Each peach pear plum, Jake spies Tom Thumb.'

In the follow-up sessions scribe the retelling into the prepared Big Book and ask each child to illustrate their contribution. Once the book is completed, use it for future 'shared book experience' reading sessions. The children can either read the story together or take turns to read their part out in turn.

Suggestion(s) for extension

In subsequent re-readings children's attention can be drawn to identifying initial letters of the characters' names by saying, for example: 'What sounds/letters does "baby bunting" start with?' This can be developed by introducing the idea of 'I spy with my little eye, someone beginning with "b". Let's look through the book and see if we can find him.' Write 'b' on the flip chart so the children can refer to it as they look through the book. This will inevitably draw the children into discussions about the initial letters of the other characters in the book.

Suggestion(s) for support

Some children will only manage to name a character or object, eg. 'a bear' or 'Bo-Peep'. They will gain much from further sharings and retellings of the story and further practice at using the 'I spy...' phrase. These children will also benefit from further 'I Spy' activities using other picture books, such as Eric Hill's *Where's Spot?* (1980, Heinemann). *Where's Spot?* is particularly helpful as it is a straightforward hide-and-seek book which follows a simple question and answer format. In addition, different animals are hidden in a predictable fashion under the flaps in the book.

Assessment opportunities

The children's growing understanding of the concept 'I Spy' should be recorded – that is, looking, identifying and naming an object or character in the book. It will be useful to note how they phrase their turns and how they participate in re-readings of the collaborative story. If children identify initial letters of characters' names this should be noted.

Opportunities for IT

Children could use a word processor to create a more polished final version of the Each Peach I Spy book. Once the initial activity has been done children could type in their own lines, for example 'Each peach, pear plum, Jake spies Tom Thumb'. A master format could be set up in advance by the teacher so that the pages were similar in appearance. Once printed, children could illustrate their page and the complete book could be bound for future use. The activity would be useful for introducing the use of capital letters for the names used.

Alternatively children could use a concept keyboard linked to the word processor so that the words for 'each, peach pear plum' etc and other names were already available for the children without a need to type them in at the keyboard. Framework software like My World could also be set up in a similar way so that the key words were available for children to pick up with the mouse and position on the page. Other words and names could be typed in at the keyboard.

Display ideas

The original version of *Each Peach Pear Plum* can be displayed and a tape of the story provided for the children to listen to. The children's version can also be placed in the book corner and a tape made to accompany it.

Aspects of the English PoS covered

Speaking and listening – 1c; 3b.
Reading – 1c; 2b.

'I SPY' NAME GAME

To develop alphabetic knowledge with a particular focus on initial letter names and sounds.
†† *Small group or whole class.*
🕑 *15–20 minutes.*

Previous skills/knowledge needed

Children should all be able to recognise their first names. Some may know the initial letter name and/or initial sound of their name. They should have had experience of playing the conventional version of 'I Spy' and, over time, have been encouraged to find their names in many different contexts, for example on their coat peg label, on their 'tidy drawer', on their books, on work displayed in the classroom, and so on.

Key background information

Among the phonic knowledge key skills identified in the National Curriculum Programme of Study is that of understanding the 'relationship between print symbols and sound patterns' and particularly 'identifying initial and final sounds in words'. Initial sounds are more easily heard and identified than final sounds, so this provides a logical starting point for developing the children's existing knowledge. Games such as 'I Spy' help to develop awareness of the '"within-syllable" aspects of rhyme and alliteration' so necessary in early literacy. (Bryant, P. (1993) 'Phonological aspects of learning to read' in *Teaching Literacy: Balancing Perspectives* (ed) Beard, R., Hodder & Stoughton)

Preparation

Make a set of name cards for all the children in the class (laminated for durability). If appropriate, each name card can be illustrated by a photograph of the child. The activity is best carried out on a table which has plenty of space.

Resources needed

Name cards.

What to do

Explain to the group that you will be playing 'I Spy' but in a slightly different way from usual, as you will be using the class name cards for the game. First of all place the name cards face up on the table one at a time and ask the children to help read out the names (ensure that the cards are laid down in such a way that they are the right way up for the children to read). During this part of the activity involve everyone so that they get a chance to identify names. If any names are not identified, read each one for the group as the card is laid down and draw attention to the initial letter and/or sound. Encourage the children to make connections where possible with other names that start with the same sound/letter.

Once all the cards are on the table start playing 'I Spy', picking one of the children's names, eg. 'I spy with my little eye, a name beginning with "W".' (William.) If William recognises his name from the 'W' clue, he should then be invited to find and pick up his card. Then it is his turn and so on. Continue the game until all the cards have been identified and removed from the centre of the table.

The alphabet

To conclude, let each child take turns to replace the pile of cards one at a time face up on the table. The child sitting to his/her right should be asked to read the card that has just been put down before taking his/her turn, so that the children begin to read each other's names.

Suggestion(s) for extension

For those who coped well with the game, it could be played again focusing this time on the final letter, eg. 'I spy with my little eye, a name ending in "m" (sound).' If 'William' recognises his name, he picks up the card.

The original game will provoke much discussion if the children are dealing with several names that start with the same initial letter, eg. 'Mark', 'Meena' and 'Michelle'. In order to differentiate between these names, the game could be played by identifying the initial *and* final sound, eg. 'I spy with my little eye, a name that begins with a "M" and ends with a "k".'

Suggestion(s) for support

For very inexperienced children the set of name cards could be prepared with a photograph of the named child to provide contextual support. With these children it might also be appropriate to limit the number of cards used and to focus on specific initial letters. Adding clues such as 'it's a very short name' (eg. Tim) or 'it's got lots of letters' (eg. Sebastian) will help these children to succeed. If the group still experiences difficulty, then play a conventional game of 'I Spy' along the lines of 'I spy with my little eye, someone beginning with "C" (sound first).'

Assessment opportunities

Note who can respond to hearing the initial letter-sound of his/her name and identify his/her card. It should also be recorded if the child can identify other children's names. On subsequent occasions it will be useful to see how many more names the child can identify. In addition, they may also recognise names that start with the same initial letter-sound. Information should also be kept about children who can identify the final letter/sound in names (see 'Initial and final sounds assessment sheet – photocopiable page xxx).

Display ideas

Set up either a magnet board or flannelgraph board and make a set of children's names either with magnetic strips or velcro on the back, so that the children can play with the names and gain more practice. A notice placed by the board could change daily, inviting the children to find names starting with different letters of the alphabet and put them on the board, for example: 'Today's names all start with "a".'

Aspects of the English PoS covered

Speaking and listening – 3b.
Reading – 2b.

Reference to photocopiable sheet

As the children play the game use the 'Initial and final sounds assessment sheet' on page 110 to record each child's ability and development.

'I SPY' PEOPLE

To enable children to understand the link between the initial letter or sound and a particular object that is represented by that sound or letter.

†† *Small or large group.*

🕐 *15 minutes.*

Previous skills/knowledge needed
Children need to know the names of the people in the group. Some knowledge of initial letters would be helpful. This game is aimed at beginners, so previous experience is not necessary.

Key background information
Children need to be able to hear the sounds which make up words (phonemes) before they can begin to make the connection between the sounds of words and the printed symbols. Many children need considerable practice in this activity and focusing on the initial sound of a word is the easiest place to start.

Resources needed
Each Peach Pear Plum by Janet and Allan Ahlberg (1989, Penguin), flip chart or chalkboard.

What to do
Read through *Each Peach Pear Plum* with the children either to introduce the session or to conclude it. Alternatively, the book may have been used in a previous session (or sessions) to familiarise children with the concept of 'I Spy'. The book is particularly appropriate for this session as one of the central themes of the book is to 'spy' all the characters (see activity on page 21 '"Each Peach" I Spy book').

Explain to the group that you will be playing 'I Spy' with them, but this time they will be playing the game based on the other people in the class or group. They will be taking turns to 'spy' but must pick the name of someone present in the classroom. Check that they are familiar with the routines and rules of the game.

Start the game off in the usual way by saying, 'I spy with my little eye, someone whose name begins with... (sound of letter).' The first child to give the correct answer then takes his/her turn. The game concludes when all the children have participated.

Suggestion(s) for extension
If children are managing this activity then they could be asked to guess how many letters there are in the name and to attempt to spell the name aloud. Using the flip chart, scribe the names for the children to look at and encourage discussion about similarities and differences, for example in terms of letter patterns, length of words, names with similar sounds in them, and so on. The game could then be widened further to include a range of objects in the room.

When the children are familiar with the sounds of the letters, the game could be played using the letter names.

Suggestion(s) for support
Children who find the game too difficult can be supplied with clues, eg. 'She is the tallest child in the class' or 'He has green eyes'. These children can also work with a partner with whom they can confer at all stages of the game. If some children still find the activity too difficult then go back to *Each Peach Pear Plum* as an enjoyable way of helping children grasp the underlying 'hide and seek' concept of 'I Spy'. The children should be encouraged to spot the characters hidden in the illustrations.

Assessment opportunities

Through what they say, children will reveal their growing knowledge of the alphabet and their ability to link initial and final sounds (and letter names) to people's names. Note who can/cannot make these links. It is helpful also to keep a record of errors in order to establish whether similar errors arise in different activities. It will be useful to note with less able children whether they are more successful working within a more limited range of choice, in this game of 'I Spy' than they are in some of the other 'I Spy' games.

Aspects of English PoS covered

Speaking and listening – 3b.

'I SPY' KITCHEN GAME

To help children establish links between letter names and/or sounds with familiar objects.

†† *Small group.*

⏰ *15 minutes.*

Previous skills/knowledge needed

Children should be able to recognise and name the set of objects which the teacher chooses to use for the game. Minimal alphabet knowledge is needed. Children should all have had some experience of naming objects and seeing print linked to them. Their understanding of the link between print and objects may still be developing. Children should have had experience of looking at catalogues including published materials such as Janet and Allan Ahlberg's *The Baby's Catalogue* (1984, Penguin).

Key background information

Children need to be able to hear the sounds which make up words (phonemes) before they can begin to make the connection between the sounds of words and the printed

symbols. Many children need considerable practice in this activity and focusing on the initial sound of a word is the easiest place to start. The use of letter cards (or wooden letters) introduces the letter symbol into this activity.

Preparation

Decisions as to selecting a category of objects, how many objects and which alphabet letters to focus on is left to the class teacher's discretion. It is important to select objects that start with different letters. To play this variation of 'I Spy' a set of familiar objects or pictures is used, in this case objects found in the kitchen. (Objects found in the classroom, objects found in the supermarket, and so on could be substituted if more appropriate.) Photocopiable pages 111 and 112 give a set of pictures of kitchen objects which should be copied on to card, laminated, cut out and stored safely.

Resources needed

The set of kitchen object picture cards (see 'Preparation'), placed in an envelope, or a set of kitchen objects placed in a bag; a set of letters (wooden, magnetic or on card) to represent the initial letter of each selected object (the rest of the alphabet should be kept in reserve for extension activities), 'Alphabet knowledge record sheet' from photocopiable page 113.

What to do

Explain to the children that you will be playing 'I Spy' with some objects (or picture cards). Explain the essential rules of 'I Spy', then, one by one, produce each object (or card) and place it on the table. Ask the children to name them as you do so. Name any objects with which children are unfamiliar, adjusting to their preferred names, eg. 'pan' for 'saucepan'. Lay the set of letters on the table. Explain that the first letter of the name of each of the objects starts with one of the accompanying letters. Start the game off with 'I spy with my little eye, something beginning with 'p' (letter sound) (Pan). If a child provides the correct response, ask him to identify the letter 'p' from the set of letters provided. The letter is then placed next to the object. The child then takes his turn to select an object for the others to identify. The game concludes when all objects have been identified and have had a letter linked to them.

The game can be played in the same way using the letter names once children are familiar with the letter sounds.

Suggestion(s) for extension

Children who are confident with the basic game can then be asked to link *all* the initial letters to the complete set of objects. They can also be asked to organise the objects into alphabetical order. Looking at the letter cards, they could be asked to identify missing letters. (Have the complete set of alphabet cards ready to support them as they do this.) Children could go on to 'spy' different sets of objects, such as sweets or snacks.

Suggestion(s) for support

To ensure that all the children experience success, they could be paired up when it is their turn to say 'I spy...' This should enable them to pick the appropriate letter to go with their chosen object. It may be necessary to get them to try out their choice on the teacher first. Again, when they are choosing the letter to go with the object that has just been guessed, guidance and additional clues may be needed. If the child makes an error the rest of the group should be encouraged to help him find the correct answer.

Assessment opportunities

Note who can/cannot link letters to objects. A record should be kept of all correct responses and also of errors, eg. mistaking 'c' for 'k' (sound) or 'c' for 'o' (graphic). The accompanying 'Alphabet knowledge record sheet' on photocopiable page 113 should be used over time to record children's growing alphabetic knowledge and to diagnose the nature of errors.

Opportunities for IT

Children could use a concept keyboard linked to a word processor to play the game and record their alphabet ability at the same time. The teacher would need to create a concept keyboard overlay with pictures of the kitchen items and their names in words. These could be distributed with pictures on the left-hand side of the overlay and the words on the right-hand side. Children can then link the picture with its name by pressing the picture of the object and its word name. When the picture and its corresponding name is pressed the two words should appear on the same line of the word processor screen. The printed version could be used by the teacher to assess the child.

A similar approach could be taken with framework software like My World where pictures of the objects can be matched with their names by dragging them on to the working area of the screen.

Display ideas

The set of objects or pictures could be displayed with the accompanying set of letters. This will provide children with additional opportunities to practise their knowledge, preferably working with a partner. Name cards (illustrated if appropriate) could also be provided to support the children.

Aspects of the English PoS covered

Reading – 2b.

Reference to photocopiable sheets

Use photocopiable pages 111 and 112 to make a set of kitchen object picture cards. An alphabet knowledge record sheet (photocopiable page 113) is also provided to record children's knowledge of the alphabet. It can also be used as a general record of a child's growing confidence in recognising, reading and using the alphabet.

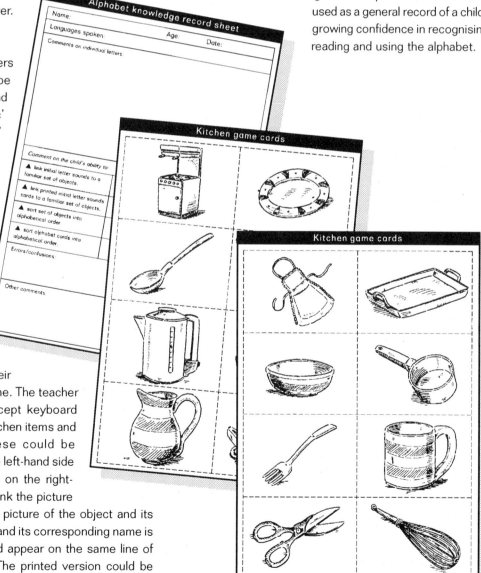

◢ HAPPY NAME FAMILIES

To identify and sort names into sets according to their initial letter.

†† *Small group activity suitable for four players.*

🕐 *15–20 minutes.*

Previous skills/knowledge needed

Children should be able to recognise their first names and have some knowledge of other people's names, including family, friends, other children in the school, and so on.

Key background information

Drawing children's attention to the fact that other people's names can start with the same initial letter as their own will encourage them to look for similar connections with other initial letters and other people's names. Talking about initial letters and letter-sounds enables the teacher to point out inconsistencies, for example where the written letter is the same but the sound is different as in 'Amy' and 'Amrit', or 'Gemma' and 'Glen'.

Preparation

Make a pack of 'Happy Name Families' cards with the children over a number of previous sessions, using the card templates provided on photocopiable page 114. For four players a minimum of eight different letter families should be made. Copy the photocopiable page eight times and write an alphabet symbol in the top right-hand corner of each card (a different letter for each page). Ask the children to write a name on to each card, beginning with the letter in the corner of that card, and illustrate it with a happy face. Completed sheets should be mounted on to card and, if possible, laminated, before being cut into individual cards. It will help the children in sorting the cards if the appropriate alphabet symbol is written in the top right corner of the card.

Resources needed

A pack of 'Happy Name Families' cards (see 'Preparation'), photocopiable page 115 (Assessment sheet).

What to do

Tell the children that they are going to play a game similar to 'Happy Families' and ask them to explain the rules to you. If they cannot, you will need to explain the rules as follows:

▲ The teacher deals the cards to all the players.

▲ Each player looks at the cards in her hand and sorts them, putting together all those of the same family (that is, those beginning with the same letter).

▲ Each player then decides which family she wishes to collect.

▲ The player to the left of the dealer (in this case the teacher) asks one other player, 'Please, do you have one of the "A" (or other letter) family?'

▲ If the player has the card requested, he must pass it to the one who asked.

▲ The recipient of the card must then say, 'Thank you.' If he forgets to say 'Thank you,' he may not keep the card; if 'Thank you,' is said, the card is added to the family in that player's hand and this player has another turn.

▲ If the person asked does not have the card, he must say, 'Sorry, I don't have one of the "A" (or other letter) family.'

▲ The turn then passes to this player.

The game continues in this manner until all families have been collected by the various players. For players who are new to the game, it would be a good idea to play at least one full game with the cards on view, so that the teacher can offer guidance and advice on how to play.

To conclude, each family could be placed in alphabetical order in the centre of the table, with the teacher calling out each family in order.

Suggestion(s) for extension

For children who are confident with the alphabet, a full set of 'Happy Name Families' cards can be used. Once the children have made all their families they can work together to make a Name Alphabet. The child with the 'A' family selects one of their cards followed by the child with the 'B' family who places one of their cards next to the first child's choice, and so on until a complete Name Alphabet has been made. If they wish, three more Name Alphabets can be made. Alternatively, a back to front Name Alphabet can be made by starting at 'Z' and working in reverse to 'A'.

Suggestion(s) for support

For children who are in the early stages of reading names, the game could be limited to working with four letters with which they are familiar. It might be helpful for these children to adapt the game so that it can be played as 'Pairs'.

The alphabet

Reference to photocopiable sheet

Photocopiable page 114 provides a template for making a pack of cards. It is recommended that the sheet is mounted on to card for strength and then laminated once it has been filled in and illustrated with a happy face. It will help the children if the appropriate alphabet symbol is written in the top right-hand corner of the card.

Photocopiable page 115 provides a framework for assessment. It can be adapted as a tick-list if required.

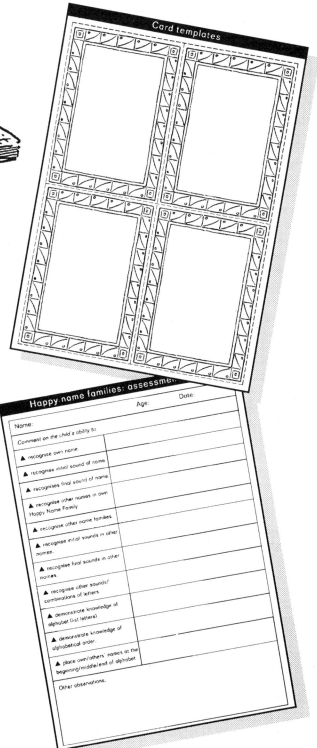

Alternatively, by making two identical name cards using known names to the children, the game can also be played as 'Snap'. Their attention should be drawn to the initial letters and also to alphabetical order.

Assessment opportunities

Note the initial letters that the child can identify and the growing number of names recognised. Note whether the child is able to help other children complete sets of families, spotting similarities and differences. See if the child is aware of the order in which the families should be packed up at the end of the game. With children using the full set of alphabet cards it should be possible to note the extent of their alphabet knowledge. Encourage the children to discuss where letters come in the alphabet – beginning, middle and end. See if they can identify where their initial letter fits within the alphabetic order. Use photocopiable page xxx to help with recording your assessments.

Display ideas

Setting up either a magnet board or flannelgraph and providing a set of 'Happy Name Families' cards with either a magnetic strip or velcro on the back gives the children further opportunities to play the games. A different focus can be provided on a daily basis by providing a series of notices, for example: 'Can you find the "F" family and put them on the board? Which family should come next? Put them on the board too.'

Aspects of the English PoS covered
Reading – 2b.
Writing – 2d.

ALPHABET SOUP – A CLASS ALPHABET

To develop familiarity with the letters of the alphabet and their sequence.

†† *Whole class or small groups.*

🕐 *30 minutes. (This activity could be split into two sessions: (1) collecting the children's ideas for the alphabet and making their contribution to the frieze; (2) a shorter follow-up session where they construct the display and learn how to use it.)*

Previous skills/knowledge needed

Children should have some experience of reciting the alphabet and seeing the alphabet in a variety of formats, for example a frieze on the wall, alphabet books, magnetic letters. They should also have some knowledge of linking the letters/sounds of the alphabet to objects and of sequencing the letters.

Key background information

Children need to learn that the sounds of the spoken language are represented in writing by the set of symbols that are the letters of the alphabet. In English, there is often not a direct sound/symbol correspondence, but the starting point for writing is nevertheless a knowledge of these alphabet symbols.

Preparation

Prepare an area of the wall for the 'Alphabet Soup' frieze. Cut out a large cooking pot or soup bowl shape as the background of the frieze. Prepare (that is, draw and label) the first item for the soup, for example 'apples', and place it on the frieze. The complete alphabet could be placed across the top or bottom of the frieze for the children to refer to.

Resources needed

Card/paper, art materials, writing materials, cookery magazines and books, an alphabet that is visible to the whole class, a flip chart with the alphabet written on it or a magnet board with the letters of the alphabet in sequence, published alphabet books (optional).

What to do

Establish the children's existing knowledge of the alphabet and discuss with them why it is important to know it.

As a whole group recite or sing the alphabet through and/or read a published alphabet book. Explain that today they will be making a 'crazy alphabet' called 'Alphabet Soup'. Draw their attention to the basic frieze already on the wall. What they are going to do is to think of different foods which could go into the 'Alphabet Soup' which later on they will draw and label to put into the cooking pot/soup bowl. Show them the 'apples' example which has already been positioned on the display.

In order to make the perfect 'Alphabet Soup' it will be necessary for the children to think of an item of food for *every* letter of the alphabet. Brainstorm with the children some foods that they would like to put in the soup. Then, using the flip chart or magnet board, work through the alphabet and scribe their suggestions. Use recipe books to support them. Emphasise the letter name/sound as each

The alphabet

FOOD ABC

Almonds	Chocolate	Hamburgers	Margarine	Peas	Sandwiches	Walnuts
Apples	Coconuts	Honey	Marmalade	Potatoes	Sardines	Watercress
Apricots	Courgettes	Hot cross	Mayonnaise	Quails	Soup	Watermelon
Artichokes	Dates	buns	Mushrooms	Quiche	Spaghetti	Wholemeal
Asparagus	Doughnuts	Ice-cream	Nectarines	Quince	Toast	bread
Avocado	Dumplings	Jacket	Noodles	Radishes	Tomatoes	Yoghurt
Bacon	Eels	potatoes	Nuts	Raisins	Tuna	Yorkshire
Basil	Eggs	Jam	Oil	Raspberries	Turkey	pudding
Bananas	Fish	Jelly	Olives	Ravioli	Turnips	Zabaglione
Beans	Flour	Ketchup	Omelette	Rice	Vegetables	Zest
Biscuits	Fruit	Kippers	Onions	Risotto	Vinegar	
Bread	Gingerbread	Lasagne	Oranges	Roast beef	Wafers	
Butter	Gooseberries	Lemons	Oysters	Salad		
Cabbage	Grapefruit	Lentils	Paella	Salami		
Cake	Grapes	Lettuce	Pancakes			
Carrots	Gravy	Macaroni	Parsley			
Cheese	Haddock	Mackerel	Pasta			
Chips	Ham	Mangoes	Peaches			

item is decided upon. Organise the children as appropriate – most children will work alone, although it may be more supportive for those who might have difficulty to work in pairs – in order to produce their labelled item of food for the frieze. Ensure by the end of the session that all items are ready to be displayed. The table shows a list of foods beginning with each letter of the alphabet which you may find helpful.

To conclude, the 'ingredients' for the 'Alphabet Soup' should be attached to the frieze (if possible, use velcro or 'Blu-Tack' so that they can be detached for future use). Involve the children in deciding the alphabetical sequence as the items are positioned. Ask questions such as, 'Which letter comes after "C"? (Yes, it's "D".) What word did we find? (Doughnuts ...)' and so on. Use the alphabet which forms part of the display as a point of reference against which the children can check their decisions.

Suggestion(s) for extension

Some children will already have a thorough working knowledge of the alphabet and its sequence. These children can be provided with their own materials, for example a blank

zigzag book, in which they can concoct their own version of 'Alphabet Soup' independently. These children can also be encouraged to think of more than one item for each letter of the alphabet and be shown how to order the words by looking at the second letters, eg. 'bananas'; 'beetroot'.

On completing their 'Alphabet Soup' book they could then be encouraged to write an instructional text to accompany their book, which could use the language of 'recipe' writing and explain in detail (including quantities) how the soup is to be made. The book should list the ingredients in strictly alphabetical order. The resulting book should provide entertaining reading material for the book corner. (Roald Dahl's *George's Marvellous Medicine* (1981, Jonathan Cape) could prove an inspirational stimulus for this part of the activity.)

Suggestion(s) for support

Children who have very little knowledge of the alphabet could be allocated their item for the 'Alphabet Soup' by utilising the first letter of their own name, for example, Christopher could be asked to provide 'carrots'. The child can be supported in their choice of item either by referring back to

the brainstorm undertaken at the start of the session or by using familiar published alphabet books. It may be necessary to scribe the label to accompany their picture. They will also need help when placing their word on the frieze, with questions like, 'Is your letter near the beginning of the alphabet? Which letters is it next to? Let's look at the wall alphabet to find out. Run your finger along until you find the letter "C".'

Assessment opportunities

Through their oral contributions children will reveal their knowledge of the alphabet, their growing understanding of the sequence of the letters, knowledge of initial letters/sounds and their ability to think of words that start with specific letters of the alphabet. More experienced children will be demonstrating their ability to identify more than one word for each letter and whether they are able to sort these further by looking at second letters.

Opportunities for IT

Children could use a word processor and work in pairs to type in and print out their items of food for the alphabet soup. This could be used as an assessment activity following similar word processing activities to see how independently the children can work at entering and printing out their work for the display. More able children might be shown how to change the font or the size of the text to make their label fit the paper, or screen.

Groups of children could create their own complete alphabet soup using a word processor. They could type the alphabet down the side of the screen. This would involve pressing the RETURN key to make sure each letter started on a new line and then typing in the names of the foods as they think of them. They will need to be shown how to move the cursor around the screen so that they can move to the various letters as children think of words to fit. This would also be a good opportunity to show children that when their work disappears off the top of the screen it is still there and how they can retrieve it. The final list could be printed out and displayed with other Alphabet Soup work.

Children could also use a word processor to create their Alphabet Soup recipe. They should be given opportunities to originate their work on the computer rather than copying hand-written work. An adult scribe/typist may help to speed up the first entry at the keyboard. Copies can then be printed out for reading and re-drafting away from the computer and then final editing and organisation back at the keyboard. Children may also begin to discuss how to present their work, using appropriate fonts and texts styles to make it look more interesting to the reader. This activity may involve the children in saving copies of their work as they go along, especially if it cannot be completed in a single session. The final recipe can be printed out and used in the classroom display.

Display ideas

The 'Alphabet Soup' frieze which the children have made should be used as an interactive display (see, for example, the following activity 'Using Alphabet Soup').

Aspects of the English PoS covered

Reading – 2a.
Writing – 2d.

USING ALPHABET SOUP

To familiarise children with the letters of the alphabet and their sequence.

†† *Small or large group activity*

🕐 *15–20 minutes.*

Previous skills/knowledge needed
Children should have some experience of using the alphabet and linking words with each letter. They should have helped to construct the 'Alphabet Soup' frieze (see the previous activity), and should have had some previous experience of sequencing the alphabet. If the 'Alphabet Soup frieze has not been made, a selection of the food items from the table on page xx should be written on to cards – one item for each letter of the alphabet.

Key background information
Children need to learn that the sounds of the spoken language are represented in writing by the set of symbols that are the letters of the alphabet. In English, there is often not a direct sound/symbol correspondence, but the starting point for writing is nevertheless a knowledge of these alphabet symbols. A knowledge of alphabetical order will be essential later on if children are to be able to find words in a dictionary, or books in a library.

Preparation
None for the main activity. The support activity would need teacher-made 'Alphabet Soup' cards, each bearing the name and a picture of the item from the soup. These could be drawn or cut from magazines, stuck on to card, and then laminated, if possible.

Resources needed
'Alphabet Soup' frieze (made in the previous activity), picture cards of the items of food (for support), cooking pot or large plastic bowl (for support).

What to do
Draw the children's attention to the recently made 'Alphabet Soup' frieze. First, ask the children to identify their words on the frieze by asking questions such as, 'What was the first thing that we put into our "Alphabet Soup"?' Then, encourage them to identify the initial letter/sound of their word by saying, for example, 'What letter/sound does "banana" start with?' Do this in the correct alphabetic sequence and focus the children's attention on the beginning, middle and end of the alphabet.

Encourage the children to identify the letters that sit next door to each other, for example by saying, 'What word comes after "banana"?... Yes, "carrot". "Carrot" begins with...' The children can be encouraged to recite the 'Alphabet Soup' alphabet by saying, '"Apple" starts with "a", "banana" starts with "b"...' and so on. They may also like to try reciting the alphabet in reverse.

Suggestion(s) for extension
Mix up the words of the 'Alphabet Soup' and ask the children to re-order them. Children who show confidence can find out how many words there are in the 'Alphabet Soup' alphabet. They can also try writing the alphabet in reverse. If they have been introduced to the terms vowel and consonant, they can list the words that start with vowels and then the words which start with consonants.

Suggestion(s) for support
Children who find working with the frieze difficult might work more successfully with the 'Alphabet Soup' cards and, in a small group, practise sorting them into the cooking pot in the correct sequence. They will have the large frieze to refer to for extra support.

Assessment opportunities
Note children's knowledge of the sequence of the alphabet and their awareness of whether letters come at the beginning, middle or end.

Opportunities for IT
The teacher could prepare a concept keyboard overlay with all of the Alphabet Soup words on them. If this is then linked

to a word processor children can be asked to put the words into alphabetical order. They can do this by simply pressing each word so that it appears on the screen. The final version can be printed out and could be used for assessment purposes. A similar activity could be done with framework software like My World where the Alphabet Soup words are arranged around the working area and children drag them onto the working area using a mouse. They can easily reorganise words if they get them in the wrong order. In both activities the full alphabet could be printed on the concept keyboard overlay or the screen to assist children.

More able children could be introduced to the 'drag and drop' facilities on some mouse driven word processors so that they can pick up words and move them into the correct order. The teacher could prepare the jumbled list in advance using the word processor and children could put it into alphabetical order. The final list could be printed out. Children will need to be shown how to use the RETURN key to separate words on to new lines as they move them around the screen.

Display ideas
Children should be encouraged to continue using the wall display. The 'Alphabet Soup' cards and bowl can be placed on a table as an alternative activity for the children to use.

Aspects of the English PoS covered
Reading – 2a.

◆ 'I SPY' WORD CHAIN

To raise children's awareness of initial and final sounds/letters in words. To focus on initial single consonants, vowels, initial consonant digraphs (eg. 'ch'); and initial consonant blends (eg. 'st').

†† *Small or large group activity.*

🕐 *15–20 minutes.*

Previous skills/knowledge needed
Confident knowledge of initial/final letters will be advantageous as well as experience of playing the conventional form of 'I Spy'. This game is well suited to more experienced players.

Key background information
Children need to be able to hear the sounds which make up words (phonemes) before they can begin to make the connection between the sounds of words and the printed symbols. Many children need considerable practice in this and focusing on the initial sound of a word is the easiest place to start, moving on to focus on the final sound. This version of the game should develop awareness of consonant blends and digraphs at the beginning of words and should reinforce the written forms of these.

Preparation
Write the complete alphabet vertically on the flip chart or chalkboard.

Resources needed
Flip chart or chalkboard, set of blank cards for 'word chain' (enough for all the children in the class), pens/pencils, photocopiable page 116 (record sheet).

What to do
Explain to the children that you will be playing 'I Spy' with them. Remind them of the essential rules (see 'I Spy', page xxx). First, play a round of the original game with the group and then introduce the 'word chain' variation, which is intended to help them focus on the beginnings and endings of words. Explain that, to play this version of the game, each person who correctly identifies an object is required to think of another object starting with the last letter of the first object, and so on. Start the game by saying, 'I spy with my little eye, something beginning with "c" (sound).' (Clock.) The first child to give the correct response then takes their turn. 'I

spy with my little eye, something beginning with "k" (sound).' (Key.)

To keep the game going, the children may need to widen their range of objects beyond those in the classroom and beyond the here and now. If they do this it is essential that they provide clues, for example 'You find this in the playground...' The oral version of this game concludes when everyone has had a turn.

The game can be extended and recorded by collecting responses on the flip chart or chalkboard. Prior to starting the session, list the complete alphabet vertically (one letter under the next) on the flip chart/chalkboard. As each correct response is given, the words can be written next to the appropriate initial letter of the alphabet (this can be done either by the teacher or by children as deemed appropriate). Once the game has been exhausted, use the chart to discuss which letters were used most frequently/ infrequently and why.

A further development would be to ask each child to write the word that they contributed on to a card. Collect all the cards and use these on future occasions for further practice to build a 'word chain'. The word chain cards should be illustrated to provide additional support for children who may find the decontextualised words hard to read on future occasions.

Suggestion(s) for extension
In the oral version of the game, confident children can be challenged by being asked to provide more complex phonic clues, such as at the beginning of words, by identifying initial consonant digraphs and blends for example, 'I spy with my little eye, something beginning with "ch" (letter names) and ending in "r" (letter name).' (Chair.) or, 'I spy with my little eye, something beginning with "fl" (letter names) and ending in "r" (letter name).' (Floor.)

Suggestion(s) for support
Children who find this activity difficult can be paired up with a 'word chain' partner to enable them to participate in the game. Help those children who successfully identify a word but then have difficulty in identifying the last letter by asking them to say the word aloud slowly, emphasising the final sound as in 'book'. Further clarification may then be necessary to help the child decide whether the hard 'c' sound is the letter 'k' or 'c'. Use the flip chart or chalkboard to

scribe possible alternatives. Encourage other children to participate by suggesting other words that follow the same pattern, eg. 'took'. It will also be appropriate to offer these children additional clues to assist them in successfully identifying words. This can be done by asking more able participants to provide additional information about their word (see 'Suggestion(s) for extension' above). Children who found this activity difficult should on subsequent occasions have opportunities to play with the 'word chain' game cards which have been made as part of the session (see the next activity, 'Word chain card game').

Assessment opportunities
Note who can/cannot link objects to initial sounds. A record should be made of who could/could not identify the final sound in the object that they guessed. Note the additional strategies/clues that were used to enable them to succeed. Record children's successful attempts to use initial consonant digraphs and initial consonant blends. Approximations and errors should also be recorded as they can be used to chart development.

Aspects of the English PoS covered
Reading – 2b.

Reference to photocopiable sheet
Photocopiable record sheet 116 is intended to be used to structure observations of children's use of initial and final sounds in words when playing the game. It can also be used as a more general record sheet.

WORD CHAIN CARD GAME

To provide further experience of identifying initial and final sounds/letters in words, including initial consonant blends and digraphs.

†† *Small group/pairs.*

🕐 *10–20 minutes.*

Previous skills/knowledge needed

Children should have some experience of 'can you go' type card games and some awareness of initial and final letters/sounds in words.

Key background information

Children need to be able to hear the sounds which make up words (phonemes) before they can begin to make the connection between the sounds of words and the printed symbols. Many children need considerable practice in this and focusing on the initial sound of a word is the easiest place to start, moving on to focus on the final sound. This version of the game should develop awareness of consonant blends and digraphs at the beginning of words and should reinforce the written forms of these.

Preparation

If you have not already done so, play the 'I Spy Word Chain' game (see previous activity). Make a set of cards, laminated if possible, on which are written the words used in this game, together with an illustration of the object, where possible. If 'I Spy Word Chain' has not been played, you should compile a set of word cards for the chain.

Resources needed

A set of laminated 'I Spy Word Chain' cards previously made by the class or the teacher.

What to do

If they have played 'I Spy Word Chain' remind the children of the game that they played recently and show them the cards that were made. Explain that they will be playing the game again, but this time using the cards. If this previous game has not been played, the teacher-made set of cards should be introduced. Ask one child to shuffle the cards and then ask another to deal them out face down in piles except for the 'start' card which is placed face up in the middle of the table. (The 'start' card will be the first word that the teacher used to commence the original 'I Spy Chain Game' if this has been played.) Tell the children that the object of the game is to rebuild the word chain. In order to start they must take turns to see if they can find the correct word to follow the word on the table. Ask them to suggest how they might go about doing this. Encourage them to spread their words out face up in front of them in order to help them succeed in their explanation. The key principle which they need to identify at this stage is that in order to find the next word in the chain, they must look at the *initial* letters on their word cards and at the *final* letter of the 'start' card. The children should then take turns until the game is completed and the word chain has been made. Due to the fall of the cards, children may need to say 'pass' if they cannot take their turn.

As the game progresses they may decide that there is a 'weak link' in the chain, when there are two or more words that start with the same letter. They may decide to play a card that 'breaks' the chain, but only realise this later on. If this happens, encourage the children to go back and make necessary alterations in order to complete the chain. This will involve looking at final letters in order to confirm their decisions.

train   nose   elephant

consonant blends and digraphs this should also be recorded. Where appropriate, direct questions may be asked about words as the game is being played, for example 'What sound do the first two letters of "broom" make?' Alternatively, the child could be asked, 'Can you tell me which two letters make the "br" sound in "broom"?'

Display ideas
The set of word chain cards could have either magnetic strips or velcro put on the back of them so that the children can use them independently on a magnet board or flannelgraph. A fresh word chain could be started on the wall of the classroom and the children encouraged to add to it when they think of a new word.

Aspects of the English PoS covered
Reading – 2b.
Writing – 2d.

Reference to photocopiable sheet
Photocopiable page 117 is designed as a 'master' record sheet to enable teachers to insert the appropriate combinations of letters for the 'chain' that they wish to assess. This sheet is intended to assist in tracking the contribution of the whole group of children during the 'Word chain card game' activity. Fill in the 'Word' column as the activity progresses, noting the name of each child who plays a word chain card and the order that the cards are played. Observations about phonic strategies used by the children, including errors and self-corrections, should be noted. If necessary, comment on the degree of assistance given.

Suggestion(s) for extension
Those who found the game easy could be asked on subsequent occasions to play the game 'solo' to see if they can complete the chain without peer group interaction or adult support. Once the children show confidence, subsequent 'group' games could involve the children playing their cards in the strict order that they have been dealt and keeping the cards face down in their pile until needed. If the card they turn up does not fit the chain they should say 'pass' and lay the card face up on the table in front of them (to fit it in later on). As the game progresses and they see the opportunity to play their card, they should do so on the next available turn. This strategy should keep the game going.

Suggestion(s) for support
For those who find the conventional game difficult, it is suggested that their set of cards be laid out in front of them throughout the game. This will make it easier for teacher/peer support and guidance. Encourage the children to look systematically through the cards in order to select the card that they need. Offer supportive suggestions. For example, if the word the child is trying to build on to is 'broom', the teacher might say, 'Look through your cards for a word starting with "m",' to draw the child's attention to the initial letter/sound. On subsequent occasions these children could work in small groups to make word chains with a smaller number of words and then play with the cards that they make to consolidate the activity and increase their confidence.

Assessment opportunities
Records should be made of those children who can/cannot identify initial and final letters/sounds of the words in the chain. A note should be made of the letters/sounds that they can identify. If children demonstrate knowledge of initial

Word chain card game: record sheet		
Date:		
Word	Child's name	Observations

WRITING THE ABC

To help children to write the alphabet and use it purposefully.

†† *Whole class (for first part of activity), then small groups separately working on their lists.*

🕐 *20–30 minutes.*

Previous skills/knowledge needed

Children should have some knowledge of the letters of the alphabet and their sequence. They should have seen their names listed in alphabetical order and have experience of making lists of names, for example for birthday party invitations. They should have heard the class list being called

in a constant alphabetic sequence and have participated in discussions about whose name comes first, last, next to one another, before, after. They should also have experience of the whole class being lined up in alphabetical order (see also 'Order! Order!' on page 44).

Key background information

Early experience of alphabetical order in the classroom is invariably the class register. This is the foundation for developing knowledge of alphabetical order, which will be essential to enable children to use reference materials, including dictionaries.

Preparation

Prepare alphabet strips by writing the letters of the alphabet on to long strips of paper. These can be attached to the children's tables, or to the wall, at eye-level, in the same way that number lines are used.

For the extension activity, small booklets will be needed and these can be made by folding A4 paper in half and stapling or sewing the fold.

Take photographs of each member of the class and label these with names (these will have many uses in other activities).

Resources needed

Alphabet strips, a class list of first names (for children to refer to if necessary), a photograph of each child, labelled with their name (for support), writing materials, small books for registers (for extension and support activities).

What to do

Talk with the class about keeping a class list. Talk about whose name comes first/last/in the middle and so on. Ask where the children's names are located, for example: 'Whose name is next to yours?' Remind the class about occasions when they have sorted themselves out and stood in alphabetical order, (see, for example, 'Order! Order!' on page 44). Run through the alphabet and, using the class list for reference, discuss which letters of the alphabet are represented by the class and which are not. Ask the children to identify any members of the class whose first name starts with the same letter as their own.

Use the class list to explain how these children are sequenced (by looking at the second letter of their name). The children should then work in pairs to produce their class list, using the resources to refer to as necessary. Once their list is complete it can be used for a number of purposes, for example as a form of class register, which the child can tally

each day, or for undertaking a survey in the class such as one about favourite television programmes.

The children will probably want to re-make the list for different purposes, so putting it on the computer and making multiple copies will also be useful.

Suggestion(s) for extension

Some children who have a thorough knowledge of the alphabet and who can write the forenames list independently can go on to make a register by using surnames to determine the alphabetic sequence. These children can organise their register into weeks by ruling in columns for the days of the week (mornings and afternoons) and can use their register on a regular basis.

Suggestion(s) for support

Some children will find writing all their friends' names a laborious business. These children could ask the other children to sign their names into a book for them. At the start of the writing part of the activity they should be encouraged to write all the names they know on a piece of rough paper. They may be able to identify the initial/final sounds of some names and should be asked to try to write these down. Encourage any insights that they might make about the names, for example 'Leon's name looks like Lee's' and ask them to explain what they have noticed about the letter patterns in their names. They should be encouraged to re-read their lists and use them in purposeful ways. Others will find that using labelled class photographs first and sequencing them into alphabetical order will support them as they try to compile their list (see 'Preparation').

Assessment opportunities

The children's knowledge of writing the alphabet can be assessed by the degree of independence that they show within the activity. Some children will demonstrate that they can apply their alphabet knowledge to look at two names and decide on their order. Others will identify initial/final sounds of some names only. Some children will find difficulty in ordering the names alphabetically and may have used the set of photographs to help them.

Opportunities for IT

The teacher could set up a concept keyboard linked to a word processor. The keyboard overlay would need to have the names of all of the children in the class (or photographs) not in alphabetical order, so that when a name was pressed it appeared on the screen. Some of the concept keyboard pads could be used as a RETURN key or to move the cursor around the screen so that children can position names where they want them. The final list could be printed out.

Older or more able children could use a word processor to type their class list. If they use the named photographs they can shuffle the photos and then pick each one up in turn and decide where in their growing list the name should be typed. Children will need to be shown how to move the cursor around the screen; create spaces on the screen by pressing the RETURN key in order to make room for a new name and edit the list when they decide names are in the wrong order. Children should be encouraged to use either a 'cut and paste' or 'drag and drop' method, rather than deleting the name and entering it again in the new position. Children can save and retrieve the completed list so that they can make new copies of it at a later date.

Aspects of the English PoS covered

Reading – 2b.
Writing – 2d.

THE GREAT, BIG, ENORMOUS SHOPPING LIST

To help children memorise the sequence of the alphabet and to link the individual letters with the initial sounds of words.

†† *Small or large group.*

⏰ *30 minutes.*

Previous skills/knowledge needed

Children should have some knowledge of the alphabet and may know some of the sequence of the letters. This activity is well suited to beginners.

Children will have to have had some experience of playing games such as 'My Grandmother's Shopping Basket'.

Key background information

Knowledge of the convention of alphabetical order is essential for children in developing reference skills in order to use dictionaries, thesauruses, encyclopaedias, telephone directories, and so on. Knowledge of alphabetical order needs to become automatic as soon as possible.

must contain one item of shopping for every letter of the alphabet. At this point recite/sing the alphabet to refresh the children's memories. Ask the children how many items will be needed on the list. In order to clarify this use the alphabet frieze or book and ask the children to help count up the letters.

The other special feature of the great, big, enormous shopping list is that they must memorise it! Once the children have responded to this piece of information, explain that today there simply isn't enough time to write down such a long list. However, memorising the list is easy. Each person in the class will think of one item for the list (some children will be working in pairs which will need identifying at this point). But, before they add their item to the list, they must remind the rest of the group of the whole list, just in case somebody forgets. There is no need to worry because if they get stuck the rest of the class can help them out. The more times that they hear the list, the easier it will become to remember. Start the game off as follows: 'On our great, big, enormous shopping list we need something beginning with "a" – "apples".' Indicate who is to take their turn next and help them follow the same formula: 'On our great, big, enormous shopping list we need some "apples" and something beginning with "b" – "bananas".' The game continues until the whole alphabet has been exhausted. (The list need not be confined to food.) At the end, the whole class should recite the shopping list (1) as items and (2) by identifying the initial letter as well as the item.

Suggestion(s) for extension
Children who can carry out this activity with ease can try reciting the list in reverse order. They can also be asked to work forward or backwards from specific points in the alphabet. These children can be asked to write down the full list and illustrate it or make a fresh list.

Suggestion(s) for support
Before embarking on the game, children who lack confidence can be paired up with a more able peer. When it comes to their turn the pair must be asked to confer to ensure the child participates. Encourage these pairs to recite the list together before adding on their item. Knowing the children's existing knowledge of the alphabet, decide on the most appropriate point to draw individuals into the activity, that is at an early stage or when the alphabet reaches the initial letter of their name.

Assessment opportunities
Assess how well the children participate in reciting the alphabet and estimating the number of letters. Note their ability to recall the items as the list grows and whether knowledge of the alphabet or associating the item with the specific letter helps them sustain the sequence. Those children who could recite the list/alphabet in reverse or from

Preparation
It is essential to count up the children in the class before embarking on the activity. If the class total is over 26 then it will be necessary to pair some children up. This should be done in advance of the session. If using the carpet area, sit the children in a semi circle facing you, or in several smaller semi circles. This will help them to recognise when it is their turn in the activity.

Resources needed
An alphabet frieze and/or books published children's books such as John Burningham's *The Shopping Basket* (1983, Armada) and Pat Hutchins' *Don't Forget the Bacon* (1978, Penguin) would be useful; a shopping basket; examples of shopping lists.

What to do
Introduce the activity by reading or talking about one or both of the children's books listed above. Explain to the children that they are going to help compile a great, big, enormous shopping list. The list is special for two reasons. First of all, it

any point in the sequence should have their achievements noted. Record the level of support children required and in which specific aspects of the activity. Areas of difficulty should be recorded in children's profiles.

Opportunities for IT
Children could work in small groups to create their list using a word processor. They could load a file which contains the alphabet, each letter on a new line, and then fill in the items of the shopping list, finally printing it out when complete. As the children are bound to find some articles easier than others they will need to be able to move the cursor around the screen so that they can come back to the difficult ones later in the activity. Once they have completed the list they may wish to select different fonts and print sizes to print the list for display in the classroom.

Display ideas
A display can be created by the children each producing an illustration of their item from the shopping list. They should be encouraged to re-read it at regular intervals. A smaller version of the shopping list can be made on 26 illustrated cards which the children can use to re-create the list in alphabetical order.

Aspects of the English PoS covered
Reading – 2a.

ONE WORD ABC
To help children focus on writing each letter of the alphabet. To reinforce the idea of alphabetical order.
†† *Small group or individual.*
🕐 *30 minutes.*

Previous skills/knowledge needed
Growing knowledge of reciting the alphabet and identifying objects by their initial sound. Previous practice at writing the alphabet with some knowledge of its sequence. Children will have to have had experience of making class alphabets with the teacher and contributing ideas both spoken and written. (The content of this activity can easily be adapted to suit the interests of the older child who is still learning to read, write and memorise the alphabet.)

Key background information
Once children have become familiar with the concept of letters and have begun to be able to associate the sounds of speech with particular letters, they need to begin to write the letter symbols. For many children this will need a great deal of practice and the active involvement in making a personal alphabet book will provide an interesting context.

Preparation
Prepare a variety of sizes and shapes of blank books with the appropriate number of pages. These can be made with folded A4 or A3 paper, with a coloured paper cover, stapled or sewn along the fold. Card zigzag books might be more suitable for some children. These can be made with A1 manila card cut into strips and folded into zigzags. They should be long enough to have 13 letters on each side of the card. Alternatively, the zigzag books could be made with separate pieces of A5 card, joined together with masking tape, to create the folds.

An optional extra would be a recent photograph of each child to go on the cover of their ABC book. If possible, make a teacher's alphabet book example of 'My favourite things', with a single word written on each page, to demonstrate ideas to the children. The book should begin with a short opening phrase ('My favourite things are...') and close with a signing-off phrase ('These are a few of my favourite things!').

Resources needed
Published alphabet books, 'My favourite things' demonstration book and prepared blank books (see 'Preparation'), illustrated dictionaries, alphabet frieze, alphabet strips displayed at eye-level, pencils, pens, crayons, photocopiable page 118.

What to do
Explain to the children that they will be making their own personal alphabet books listing their favourite things, and

SPELLING AND
PHONICS KS1

that they are to be called '(child's name) ABC', for example 'John's ABC'. Show the children the published alphabet books. Ask them to recite/sing the alphabet and ask key questions, such as how many letters are there in the alphabet? Show the children your demonstration ABC book, drawing their attention to the number of pages and where the letters of the alphabet have been written on each page. Explain that the first thing to do is to label each page of their alphabet book which will require them to check the order of the letters as they go along (direct children to the resources listed above). Once the books have been alphabetised, read the children your demonstration ABC book. The following example reads almost as a poem:

John's ABC
My favourite things are...
alligators
boomerangs
cars
dogs
elephants
football
gorillas
horses
insects
jam
kangaroos
lemons
monsters
numbers
octopuses
parrots
quizzes
roundabouts
snow
telescopes
uncles
volcanoes
Wednesdays
xylophones
yo-yos
zebras
These are a few of my favourite things!

Encourage the children to brainstorm ideas with a partner before drafting their list and writing the ideas into their ABC books. The books can then be illustrated and read aloud to the class.

Suggestion(s) for extension

Some children may find their alphabet knowledge extended further by compiling a more challenging set of words for their ABC books. The theme of 'All about me', starting with the phrase 'I am...', requires the children to utilise their alphabet

knowledge first to think of adjectives to describe themselves and then to find the words in a dictionary. The brainstorming and rough draft technique will support them in this. An example is given below.

John's ABC
I am...
angry
brave
clever
dreamy
elegant
friendly
gifted
happy
intelligent
jolly
kind
lonely
marvellous
naughty
overjoyed
practical
quick
reliable
sensible
trustworthy
unusual
vague
wonderful
(e)xtravagant
young
zany
That's me! A to Z(ee)

Alternatively, these children could work with the 'My favourite things' activity but offer two words that are alliterative, eg. 'angry alligators', 'bouncing boomerangs' and so on.

Suggestion(s) for support

Some children will find a zigzag book easier to use as it avoids page turning. Children whose alphabet knowledge is developing could be asked to write all the letters that they know on a piece of rough paper before trying to make their alphabet book. They should then work systematically through the alphabet with adult support. This may involve scribing some of the letters which the child does not have the confidence to write independently. Refer to the rough paper, drawing attention to letters that the child remembered and where they come in the alphabetic sequence. Once the ABC book has been prepared these children should work with the 'My favourite things are...' prompt and should try to say words that they think would fit each letter of the alphabet. They will probably require help in locating the words in picture alphabets and some may need the words scribed for them. With a very inexperienced group, 'One word ABC' could be undertaken as a shared writing activity, with the teacher as scribe, to produce a big (A3/A2) book for shared reading.

Assessment opportunities

Photocopiable page 118 can be used to record observations of the children's abilities and development in writing the alphabet.

The children's ability to write the alphabet can be assessed when they write it in rough and/or when they write it neatly into their book. Note which children did/did not refer to the resources provided in order to achieve this. It will be useful to record the letters which the more inexperienced children were able to identify and write independently and those which they sorted out by referring to the resources. Gaps in their alphabet knowledge should be recorded so that they can be worked on systematically in future sessions. During the brainstorm activity observe the extent to which children can orally compile a set of words but also note any errors, eg. 'king' for the 'c' page. The degree of dependence/ independence in writing the items into the book should also be recorded. Finally, listen to the child read the book, which will provide opportunities for you to ask specific questions about their growing knowledge of the alphabet.

Opportunities for IT

Children could publish their individual ABC list using a word processor. They can type in the alphabet to start with, pressing RETURN after each letter so that it is spaced down the screen. Children can then type in their individual ABC, finally printing it out when complete. As they are bound to find some letters easier than others children will need to be able to move the cursor around the screen so that they can come back to the difficult ones later in the activity. Once they have completed the list they may wish to select different fonts and print sizes to print the list for display in the classroom.

Depending on the software used children could then split their list so that each letter of the alphabet is moved on to a new page. It might be possible for the teacher, or an older pupil, to do this once the list has been completed. These can be printed out and the children can illustrate each page of their individual ABC.

An alternative approach would be for the teacher to set up a format for the book, say 26 A5 pages and then place the letter of the alphabet on each page. This could be used as a master file and saved on to a disc (its a good idea to lock this file so that it cannot be over-written by another child, and to keep another copy on a separate disc... just in case!). Each child could then load this master file, enter the individual alphabet on to the pages and save it with their own name. Finally it can be printed out and the illustrations added by hand.

Display ideas

To heighten children's interest in the alphabet, make a display of published alphabet books with one or two of the children's examples included. An alternative/parallel display could include everyday printed items which are alphabetic, for example address books, a home-made class register, a card index with class names in alphabetical order, a picture dictionary, a telephone directory and so on.

Aspects of the English PoS covered

Writing – 2d.

Reference to photocopiable sheet

Photocopiable page 118 can be used to record children's development in writing the letters of the alphabet. It can also be used to record observations from other alphabet activities.

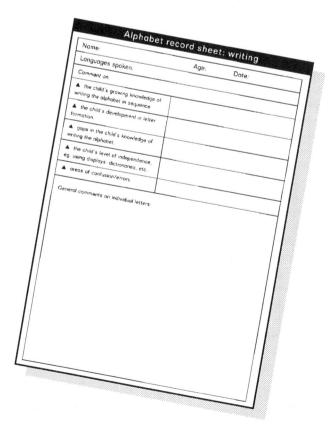

ORDER! ORDER! (WHOLE CLASS ABC)

To raise children's awareness of the alphabet and its sequence. To draw their attention to initial sounds.

†† *Whole class.*

🕐 *25 minutes.*

Previous skills/knowledge needed

Children will need some knowledge of the alphabet and its sequence. It would be useful to have had class discussions linking names and objects to their initial letter sound. Children should be able to write some or all of the letters of their name.

Key background information

Knowledge of the alphabet is fundamental to learning to read and write. In *Reading Recovery: a Guidebook for Teachers in Training* (1993, Heinemann) Marie Clay recommends that it is important to work from the 'known' with children, in other words their existing knowledge, but she also stresses the need to 'tidy up a child's knowledge of the alphabet'. By this she means that it is the teacher's responsibility to ensure that children's alphabetic knowledge does become complete and that any gaps are carefully monitored and eventually closed.

Learning to sequence the alphabet is another vital task, and children need support and practice at noticing where letters are positioned in the alphabet. When discussing alphabetical order it is necessary to use words and phrases such as 'next to', 'before', 'after', 'beginning' and 'end'. These words denote position and are sometimes difficult for children to visualise. This is why physically organising the alphabetic sequence for themselves is so important. The children can then make direct connections between the abstract and the concrete.

In order to talk about the alphabet in universal terms it is useful for children to know the letter names. Knowledge of the letter names provides children with such a metalanguage.

Preparation

A large space is needed, such as the school hall. Make an initial letter card for each child in the class on an A4 sheet of card. Write the initial letters boldly, preferably in dark pen, and large enough to be visible at some distance. Use masking tape or chalk to mark a long line along the floor, behind which the children will stand. Load the camera with a film that has enough exposures to take pictures of the whole class. Fix an alphabet frieze in a place that is visible to all.

Resources needed

Alphabetic class list, alphabet frieze, initial letter cards (see 'Preparation'), pens, chalk or masking tape, camera and film.

What to do

Sit the class in a semicircle and lay out the initial letter cards face up on the floor so that the children can read them. Explain that they will be working on sorting themselves into alphabetical order. Discuss why it is useful to know how to put their names into alphabetical order: for example, because in the classroom they frequently need to use lists of names as a checklist. Explain that, although they will start in the semicircle, they will eventually form a line along the chalk line on the floor. Ask each child in turn to say their first name. Then ask them which letter their name begins with: for example, Nicola starts with 'N'. Ask each child in turn to select their initial letter from the array on the floor and hold it. Once all the letters have been taken work through the alphabet in sequence, asking the children to stand up as they hear their letter called. As they stand up show them where they should position themselves along the chalk line in order to build the sequence. When the whole group is in alphabetical order, ask them to recite their class list alphabet, identifying their name and initial letter, such as '"A" for Alice'. They should notice who comes before/after them in the sequence and who comes first, middle and last.

To conclude, ask the group to walk slowly into a space anywhere in the room and sit down. Then explain that, when you tell them to start moving, they are all to walk slowly back to the line and arrange themselves in alphabetical order again. Try the sequence again and increase the speed with which they recite it. Finally, take individual photographs of the children holding their initial letter cards to be used for display purposes.

Suggestion(s) for extension

Using the alphabet frieze, ask the children to identify the gaps in their class alphabet and see if they can suggest people from other classes or from their families who could fill the gaps.

The alphabet

If two or more children's names start with the same letter, discuss the importance of looking at second or even third letters in order to sort out the order.

With the children sitting in a random order, play a mini-quiz to test their knowledge of the alphabet sequence. Can they remember who comes 'before', 'after', 'first' and 'last'?

The focus in the main activity is on letter names, but now ask the children to identify the first letter of their name by its initial sound. This will provide a natural opportunity to discuss similarities and differences, for example between the 'a' in 'Abbas' and the 'a' in 'Amy'. With some names, such as 'Charles', it is not helpful to identify the initial sound as 'c' because 'c' does not provide an adequate description of the initial sound of the name. In this case it is more useful to identify the initial consonant digraph 'ch'.

Suggestion(s) for support

Some children will need help in identifying the initial letter of their name. They may also need reminding about who comes before and after them in the sequence. These children will probably also need help to notice and remember the letters that precede and follow them in the sequence. Use the alphabet frieze as a reference to help the children as they talk about the alphabet.

In future lessons in the school hall, such as PE, make up a game based around the class alphabetic sequence. The phrase 'Order! Order!' could be the signal for the children to sort themselves as quickly as possible into alphabetical order.

Assessment opportunities

Note which children can/cannot link an initial letter to their name. Some children will be aware of many elements of the alphabetic sequence without seeing their classmates move and may explore this during the initial discussion. These children should be encouraged to predict the sequence. Make a note of those who can make decisions based on the second letter of names. Awareness of beginning, middle and the end of the alphabet as well as 'before' and 'after' will indicate understanding of the ordering of the alphabet. Children's knowledge of the initial sound of their own and others' names will also provide information for their records.

Display ideas

Mount the set of individual photographs as a wall display with a title saying 'Order! Order! Our Class Alphabet'. Leave gaps for any missing letters as these should be acknowledged and discussed on future occasions. Label the gaps with the missing letters and leave enough space to make additions if new children join the class. The display can be used as a reference when the class is asked to line up in alphabetical order.

Aspects of the English PoS covered

Speaking and listening – 2b.
Reading – 2a.
Writing – 2d.

TIDY THE LIBRARY

To enable children to use their knowledge of the alphabet to help them locate books by authors' surnames.

†† *Whole class or small group, then individuals.*

🕐 *40 minutes.*

Previous skills/knowledge needed

Children will need extensive knowledge of the alphabet and will need some experience of locating letters at the beginning, middle and end of the alphabetic sequence. They will have to have some knowledge of the relationship of individual letters with those positioned before and after them. By listening to the register, they will be aware that surnames are frequently used as a method of organising a large group of people. They may have noticed that libraries frequently organise books in this way also.

Key background information

Children need to know that the alphabet can serve them in many different ways. Not only do they need to be able to recite, read and write the alphabet, but they also should begin to identify wider applications of this knowledge, for example to enable them to retrieve information. An important starting point for them is to learn that by using the alphabet, librarians and teachers are able to organise large quantities of books, so that they can be found easily on future occasions. In order

to do this books are usually organised alphabetically by the authors' surnames. This activity develops these skills and helps the child to understand that the system can only be effective if books are returned to their correct position in the alphabetic sequence.

Preparation

Sort a shelf of books into alphabetical order. Select ten of the books, each by a different author, but two of them should start their surname with the same letter. Remove these books from the bookshelf. Prepare a space on another bookshelf or table to accommodate the books so that they can be laid face up in a row. Make enough copies of photocopiable pages 119 and 120 for each child in the class. Prepare alphabet strips, at least one per pair, and laminate them if possible.

Resources needed

A shelf of books in alphabetical order; ten children's books removed from the bookshelf; table or bookshelf to accommodate the books; photocopiable pages 119–122; scissors, adhesive, pencils; alphabet strips.

What to do

Starting with the whole group recite the alphabet together and then play a short quiz, asking the children about the position of letters in the alphabetic sequence, for example 'Which letter comes before "q"?' Once the correct answer is given, follow this up with 'Which letter comes after "q"?'

Continue until most children have taken a turn. Use an alphabet strip if necessary to help the children during this phase of the activity.

Next, introduce the idea of 'Tidy the library'. Ask the children to explain how they find books when they go to the library. Respond to their answers and then help them to focus on how they might find a book by a particular author, for example Roald Dahl. Again, collect their responses and then talk about the fact that fiction books in libraries are usually organised alphabetically according to the authors' surnames. Clarify any uncertainties about the terms 'authors' and 'surnames'.

Show the children the shelf of books which have been sorted into alphabetical order according to the authors' surnames. Explain that ten books have been removed from the shelf and show them to the children.

Then, remove one of the two books whose authors' names start with the same initial letter and spread the rest in a random order on the table. Ensure that all the class can see. Explain that these books need sorting into alphabetical order so that they can eventually be put back on to the bookshelf. Which book would go first? If a child provides a correct response, ask the child to explain how they made their decision. Place the book at the front of the table. Then move on to the next book and repeat the procedure, placing the second book next to the first. The children should be thinking about the alphabetic sequence and referring if necessary to one of the alphabet strips to help them. Once all the books have been sorted into a row along the front of the table, check them against an alphabet strip.

Then give each child a copy of photocopiable pages xxx and xxx. They should cut out the shapes marked on the first worksheet and stick them together to make a library bookshelf. On the second sheet they will find a set of book covers showing authors' names. The children should carefully cut these out and then decide in what order the 'books' should be tidied on to the empty bookshelf. They can use the alphabet at the bottom of the sheet to help them. They should compare their finished shelf with a partner and check whether they were correct.

Finally, ask the children (in pairs) to take turns to replace the set of books in their correct sequence among the other books on the class or library bookshelf. Then, ask the pairs to take turns to find one of the books again. They must use the author's surname to help them locate the book. Ask them which surnames came before and after. Use the alphabet strip to help them recognise how the book they were looking for was positioned in relation to its neighbours.

Suggestion(s) for extension

If the children cope well with the initial book sorting activity, use all ten of the books and repeat the activity again. This time, the children have to sort two books whose authors share the same initial letter. Ask the children which book

should come first. If a child provides the correct answer ask them to explain how they made their decision. Clarify for the group the key point, that they will need to look at the second letters of the surnames in order to assess which book comes first. The children can then move on to complete the second, more challenging, photocopiable sheet on page 121. They will need to use the 'bookshelf' from photocopiable page 119 again. Finally, ask them to select a fresh set of books from the bookshelf and to sort them into alphabetical order and then replace them in their correct positions.

Suggestion(s) for support

Some children will find the initial activity challenging and will benefit from working with a reduced number of familiar books, preferably by known authors. Working with a small group, explain that this time they will work with fewer books and that they will be using the alphabet strip to help them as they sort the books. Check that the children understand what surnames are. Ask them to tell their own surnames and then the surnames of some of their friends. Lay out the books randomly on the table and point out the authors' names. Play a short 'I Spy'-type quiz along the lines of 'I spy with my little eye, an author whose surname begins with an "H".' This will help to familiarise the children with the authors' names and draw attention to their initial letters. Ask the children to work as a group and to sort the books into alphabetical order. Once they have made their decision, they should check their answers with the alphabet strips. Use terminology such as 'beginning', 'middle', 'end' or 'next to' and 'after'. Clarify any errors, and let the children complete photocopiable page 122 in pairs, re-using the 'bookshelf' from photocopiable page 119.

Library books (3)
▲ The library has been left in a terrible mess. Can you tidy it up and put all the books back on the shelf?
Cut the books out and stick them back on the shelf. The books must go back in alphabetical order.

P. Hutchins
R. Maris
R. Briggs
J. Kerr
E. Carle
R. Dahl

▲ Use the alphabet below to help you.
A B C D E F G H I J K L M N O P Q R S T U V W X Y Z

Library books (1)
▲ The library has been left in a terrible mess. Someone has left books all over the floor. Can you clear it up and put all the books back on to the bookshelf?
Cut the books out and stick them back on the shelf. Don't forget the books must go back in alphabetical order.

J. & A. Ahlberg
P. Hutchins
A. Brown
J. Kerr
R. Dahl
E.B. White
E. Carle
R. Maris
M. Sendak

▲ Use the alphabet below to help you.
A B C D E F G H I J K L M N O P Q R S T U V W X Y Z

Assessment opportunities

In the early discussion the children will reveal their knowledge about how and why large quantities of books are organised in alphabetical order by authors' surnames. During the book sorting activity the children should comment on the position of letters in the alphabet and use appropriate prepositions to help them. Some children will understand that when two surnames start with the same letter, it is necessary to look at the alphabetic position of the second letter in both names to decide which one comes first. Note how successfully the children managed to replace the book in the correct position on the class bookshelf. Assessments can also be based on how effectively the children tackled the photocopiable sheets.

Display ideas

Ask the children to help make a display of some books that have been sorted into alphabetical order.

Aspects of the English PoS covered

Speaking and listening – 1c.
Reading – 2a.

Reference to photocopiable sheets

Photocopiable page 120 asks children to arrange a set of eight books on a bookshelf (provided on photocopiable page 119) in alphabetical order by author's surname. This is tackled by all the children, and their performance here and in the initial sorting activity determines whether they are then asked to complete photocopiable pages 121 or 122 which are more and less challenging respectively.

Rhyme & alliteration

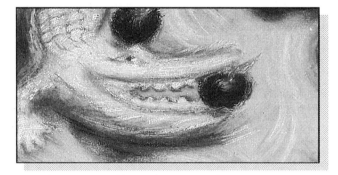

Whatever their age, children love rhyme – it has something to offer every child, from lullabies to advertising jingles. Rhyme also has an important part to play in developing children's phonic skills in reading. It is through being immersed in rhymes that children develop phonological awareness and sensitivity to the patterning of words. It is the patterning of rhyming words which is the significant factor in heightening this sensitivity.

In the initial stages of learning to read, children find working with phonemes (the smallest units of sound) very difficult partly because what they hears does not necessarily match the printed word that they see. Research has shown that children make more sense of the task of segmenting words if they are helped to use their implicit knowledge of 'onset' and 'rime'. For example, a child working with the word 'stand' will break the word up into its onset 'st' and its rime 'and'. This research has important implications for the way in which the teaching of phonics is approached in the early stages.

Through experiencing the language of nursery rhymes, children are drawn to onsets and rimes in words. Alliteration is a special feature of many rhymes and this helps to focus children's attention on the initial sounds and beginnings of words.

The activities in this chapter aim to develop this sensitivity to rhyme and alliteration. There is a strong emphasis on listening to rhyme as well as looking at the graphic features in rhyme patterns.

'HUMPTY DUMPTY': LISTENING FOR RHYMES

To enable children to listen out for and identify rhyming words within familiar nursery rhymes.

†† *Small or large group.*

🕐 *20 minutes.*

Previous skills/knowledge needed

Most children will have knowledge of nursery rhymes and playground rhymes, some of which they will be able to recite/sing off by heart. It will be advantageous if the children have previously been involved in discussions using the terms 'rhyme' or 'sound patterns'. This activity is also suitable for children with little experience of rhymes.

Key background information

Preschool children's sensitivity to rhyme and alliteration is an important indicator for their future success in reading. It is important therefore to sustain and, in some cases, develop and heighten this 'phonological awareness' in the classroom. A starting point is to provide children with plenty of experience of poetry and rhyme and to ask children to listen out for and identify rhyming words. Nursery rhymes provide ideal material to analyse children's growing awareness of onset and rime. For instance, taking the word 'wall' in the nursery rhyme 'Humpty Dumpty', the initial consonant 'w' forms the 'onset' and '-all' forms the 'rime'. In addition, by being asked to create 'rhyming families' children will have their attention drawn to phonemes (the smallest unit of sound in a word). By being able to substitute phonemes as they build 'rhyming families', the children will demonstrate their awareness that it is possible to change the meaning of a word by altering a single phoneme.

This activity can be easily adapted for older children by substituting well-known poems for the nursery rhymes.

Preparation

Select the nursery rhymes to be used in the session and either write these on large pieces of card or enlarge, colour in and laminate photocopiable pages 123 and 124.

Resources needed

Flip chart or chalkboard, large poetry cards of the nursery rhymes selected for the activity (see 'Preparation'), photocopiable page 125.

What to do

Explain to the group that this session is all about 'rhymes', especially those that we can hear in nursery rhymes. Ask the children if they can explain what the term 'rhyme' means. Note initial definitions on the flip chart or board. For example, they may offer a title such as 'It's like Mary Mary...' or they may say 'words that sound the same'. See if the children can suggest some further examples, such as 'cat' and 'bat'. Ask whether they know any nursery rhymes and encourage the children to identify their favourites. List the titles on the board or flip chart and sing/recite some of them through together. Then select a nursery rhyme to work on which has a short verse and an obvious rhyme pattern, such as 'Humpty Dumpty', and display the poetry card where the children can see it easily.

Tell the children that first they will sing 'Humpty Dumpty' together. As they do so they should listen carefully for any rhyming words that they can hear in the song. When they have finished singing, ask them to tell you the rhyming words they identified and note their suggestions. The activity can then be repeated using the other well-loved rhymes.

Suggestion(s) for extension

Children who successfully identify the pairs of rhymes in 'Humpty Dumpty' can go on to work with one rhyming word from the song, for example 'wall' and suggest other words that sound similar: for instance, 'fall', 'call', 'tall', 'hall'... Ask the children whether they can hear which part of the word stays the same and which bit changes in order to create a new word (try to carry this activity out orally, in order to focus on using their ears). These children could then move on to focusing on a longer nursery rhyme, such as 'One two, buckle my shoe'.

Follow the same routine of asking the children to listen carefully in order to identify the different pairs of rhymes. Encourage them to count how many different pairs of rhymes they can hear and ask them to comment on the sound patterns that they can hear in the words. Next, choose a rhyme with which to build a 'rhyme family'. Start with a common rhyme, for example 'ten', 'hen', 'pen'. Then work with a more challenging rhyme that will have fewer family members, such as 'floor'. Some children will methodically work through the alphabet substituting the initial sound. This should be encouraged as these children are demonstrating

SPELLING AND PHONICS KS1

Growing awareness of rhyme: assessment sheet 1

Name:

Languages spoken.   Age.   Date.

Comment on:

▲ the child's knowledge of nursery rhymes and/or other rhymes.

▲ the child's growing understanding of the word 'rhyme'.

▲ the child's awareness of rhymes in 'Humpty Dumpty' (or other rhymes).

▲ pairs of rhymes the child successfully identified.

▲ whether the child could identify the part of the words that rhymed.

▲ whether the child could suggest words to build rhyme families.

▲ wheth... different... comple...

▲ wheth... change th... altering th...

▲ wheth... ran throu... alphabetic... rhyming w...

▲ areas... lack of se...

Little Jack Horner

Little Jack Horner
Sat in the corner,
Eating a Christmas pie;
He put in his thumb,
And pulled out a plum,
And said, 'What a good boy am I.'

Humpty Dumpty

Humpty Dumpty sat on a wall,
Humpty Dumpty had a great fall;
All the king's horses and all the king's men
Couldn't put Humpty together again.

One, two, buckle my shoe

One, two
Buckle my shoe.
Three, four
Knock at the door.
Five, six
Pick up sticks
Seven, eight
Lay them straight.
Nine, ten
A big fat hen.

Eleven, twelve
Dig and delve.
Thirteen, fourteen
Maids a-courting.
Fifteen, sixteen
Maids in the kitchen.
Seventeen, eighteen
Maids a-waiting.
Nineteen, twenty
My plate's empty.

their ability to work with phonemes to change the sound and meanings of words.

Finally, use a nursery rhyme which has a more varied rhyme structure, such as 'Little Jack Horner'. See if the children notice that the 'pie'/'I' rhymes are not placed consecutively in the rhyme.

Suggestion(s) for support

If the children do not respond when asked to identify the rhymes in 'Humpty Dumpty' it may be necessary to prompt by saying, for example, 'Which word sounds like "Humpty"?' It may help to provide the children with an example to start them off: '"Humpty" rhymes with "Dumpty"... "wall" rhymes with...?' Try repeating the rhyme for them, saying it aloud slowly and emphasising the key rhyming words.

A suitable follow-up rhyme which has a similar format to 'Humpty Dumpty' would be 'One, two, three, four, five...' Working orally with this rhyme will help consolidate the children's knowledge.

Assessment opportunities

Assessment will be based on what the children hear with a focus on their growing awareness of rhyme. Use photocopiable page 125 to note who can/cannot successfully hear and identify rhyming pairs of words. Some children will substitute the initial sound systematically by running through the alphabet thereby offering evidence of their alphabetic knowledge and the ability to apply it. Record any non-rhyming pairings offered by the children, such as 'wall' and 'men'. It is important to use other nursery rhymes and activities to check whether these children consistently demonstrate a lack of sensitivity to rhyme.

Display ideas

Copies of the enlarged nursery rhymes could be illustrated by the children and displayed on the wall. Alternatively, the rhymes can be used for shared reading sessions. Make a tape recording of the rhymes to accompany the texts.

Aspects of the English PoS covered

Speaking and listening – 1a.
Reading – 2a, b.

Reference to photocopiable sheets

Photocopiable pages 123 and 124 provide four nursery rhyme cards which can be enlarged, coloured and then laminated.

The record sheet on photocopiable page 125 is intended to provide evidence of children's growing repertoire of nursery rhymes, playground rhymes, jingles, poems, etc. It also aims to provide an observational framework for this activity.

◆ 'HUMPTY DUMPTY': LOOKING FOR RHYMES

To enable children to connect the sound patterns and rhymes that they can hear to the patterns of letters in print.

†† *Large or small group.*

🕑 *40 minutes. The main activity should take about 15 minutes and the small group and pair work a further 25 minutes.*

Previous skills/knowledge needed

Children should have experience of reciting/singing nursery rhymes. Discussions should have focused on the children listening for and identifying rhyming words within nursery rhymes or poems. They will need some experience of building 'word families' or 'rhyme families' orally and it will be useful if the children are familiar with the terms 'rhyme', 'sound patterns' or 'word/rhyme families'. They may also have noticed similarities and differences in the graphic features of rhyming words when looking at and talking about books.

Key background information

Knowledge of rhyme is important to children as they begin to read. Beginning readers are able to make analogies based on 'rime' to help them to read unfamiliar words. For example, if a child can read the word 'hen', they can use analogy to read the word 'ten'. The child discovers that words in the same family share common letter patterns and that these patterns frequently represent a common sound.

Preparation

Prepare enlarged poetry cards of the nursery rhymes on photocopiable pages 123 and 124. Copy photocopiable pages 126 and 127. Make a blank book and label the cover 'Rhyme Families'.

Resources needed

Poetry cards (see 'Preparation'), chalkboard or flip chart, pens, pencils, photocopiable pages 126 and 127, dictionaries, blank book for class 'Rhyme Families' collection (see 'Preparation'), alphabet frieze.

What to do

Introduce the session by singing/reciting some favourite nursery rhymes, such as 'Humpty Dumpty', 'One, two, three, four, five' and 'One, two, buckle my shoe'. Check the children's familiarity with the word 'rhyme' and then focus on one of the nursery rhymes to identify some pairs of rhymes. Once the children have identified some of the rhymes orally, scribe the rhyming pairs and rhyme families on the board or flip chart. Initially, try to focus on regular families such as 'wall', 'hall'.

Ask the children if they notice anything about the pattern of the letters in the words. The aim is that they should recognise that, by substituting the initial sound (phoneme) with a different one, a brand new word is created. By seeing the corresponding change in the initial letter in the written form (grapheme), the children will be learning an important spelling lesson. Then ask the children which part of the word remains the same and draw their attention to the constant letter pattern, in this case 'all'. Ask the children to suggest other words that belong to the same rhyming family and see if they can suggest how to spell them. Let the children take turns to write their words on the chart and also encourage them to spell the words aloud by analogy.

It is inevitable that the children will also notice that words can rhyme, even though they may look quite different in print, for example in 'Humpty Dumpty', 'men' and 'again'. To conclude the main activity, use the 'One, two, three, four, five' photocopiable page 126 which reviews the key ideas from this section and acts as an introduction to the more demanding extension activity.

Suggestion(s) for extension

The rhymes selected can become increasingly complex in order to provoke a more challenging discussion. Give each pair a copy of 'One, two, buckle my shoe' from photocopiable page 123. Encourage the children first to listen carefully and then to work together to answer the questions on photocopiable page 127. This part of the activity will be well suited to collaborative work in pairs. Before commencing

Alternatively, the children can start compiling material for the class 'Rhyme Family' book. Split the class into small groups to work on one rhyme or poem. For example, there are ten different rhymes in 'One two, buckle my shoe' which could be studied and lists compiled. It is important from an organisational angle to be aware that some of the rhymes will be more productive than others, therefore careful allocation of the rhymes is suggested. Other rhymes and poems could also be used. Some children may choose to use dictionaries to help them compile their lists. One group of children could work with the enlarged poetry cards and write 'rhyme family ' lists in neat handwriting for display purposes.

Suggestion(s) for support
Some children will take time to understand the principle that by changing a phoneme we can change a word. Recite 'Humpty Dumpty' with the group emphasising the rhyming words. Ask the children to listen to the nursery rhyme and to identify the rhyming words. Then use the enlarged poetry card and ask the group to read the rhyme through again together. Then ask the children to point out the rhyming words on the card. When they have found the rhyming words, focus on pairs of rhymes and ask questions such as, 'Do you notice something different about these two words?' If the children do not respond, phrase the question in a more direct way, for example: 'Which bit of this word "hall" looks the same as this word "ball"?' If the children fail to recognise the 'all' pattern then demonstrate some examples for them. Then encourage them to try again using either 'Humpty Dumpty' or 'One, two, three, four, five'. List the 'all' family on the board or flip chart, encouraging the group to think of rhyming words that they know. If they find this difficult, then systematically work through the alphabet, using an alphabet frieze as a point of reference, and decide which sounds to accept or reject as the list is compiled. Some teachers who wish to encourage 'word play' will want to include nonsense words as well as 'real' words in the list. To conclude, read the list through together.

this part of the session it is important to rehearse the contents of the worksheet carefully with the children. First of all, the children are asked to underline all the pairs of rhymes. Then they should try to identify one pair of words that follows exactly the same rhyme pattern. After this the children should find a pair of words that sound similar but are spelled differently, such as 'eight' and 'straight'. Finally, they should look for a pair of rhymes that are not exact in either their spoken or written form, such as 'fourteen' and 'a-courting'. Guide them to look for the part of the words that retain the constant sound pattern and to look carefully at the segment of the word which causes the change in the rhyme. Discuss with them why they think this happens.

Assessment opportunities
Use photocopiable page 128 to assess the children's awareness of how 'rhyme families' are constructed, that is whether they notice changes in the 'onset' part of the word when they see the word in print. Record the degree of confidence and independence that they demonstrate when compiling their own 'rhyme families'. It will be useful to note which children refer to the alphabet frieze or dictionaries to help them work systematically and those that prefer to use a random approach. Some children will be able to construct their lists by making the substitutions by analogy. Look out for children who demonstrate increased confidence in their ability to spell words that belong to word families. It is helpful to list systematically the rhymes which the children have

worked with. Children's growing ability to discriminate between words that are not exact rhymes should be noted, as should their growing knowledge of words that have the same rhyme but are different in their graphic representation.

Opportunities for IT
Children could write their word family lists using a word processor and discuss how to select appropriate fonts and styles for displaying the list to the rest of the class. Different pairs of children could work on different pages of a class rhyme book, possibly centred on 'One two buckle my shoe'. Each pair could be given a different rhyme to explore and they could type in their new words and rhymes onto their own page. This would involve the children in moving around the document to their page, entering and editing their text and saving the document onto disc. The completed book could be printed out and bound for further use in the class.

If the class has access to a talking word processor the children can experiment by looking for rhymes and checking the words they have typed in to see if they rhyme with their starting word. Children will need to be shown how to select the 'talk' option for both the starting word and their rhyming word and move to cursor to the words to be checked. Children could also be introduced to the spelling checker to see if the words they have created are 'real' or made up words. The completed list could be printed for display purposes.

Display ideas
A display could be set up using one of the enlarged poetry cards as the centrepiece. The 'rhyme families' that have been compiled that relate to the rhyme can then be displayed around it. A class 'Rhyme Family' book could be compiled and added to as new rhymes are worked with.

Aspects of the English PoS covered
Speaking and listening – 1a; 2b.
Reading – 2b.
Writing – 2c.

[Worksheet illustrations: "How well does it rhyme? (1)", "How well does it rhyme? (2)", "Growing awareness of rhyme: assessment sheet 2"]

▲ Working with a partner, read the rhyme through. Listen carefully for the rhymes.

One, two, three, four, five,
Once I caught a fish alive,
Six, seven, eight, nine, ten,
Then I let it go again.

▲ There are four rhyming words. Can you find them? Put a circle round the words.
▲ Now, write the rhyming words. The rhyming words are:
1
2
3
4
▲ Two words have their rhyme spelled the same way. Write down the two words.
1
2
▲ Find the two rhyming words that are spelled in different ways. Write them down.
1
2

Reference to photocopiable sheets
Photocopiable pages 123 and 124 provide four nursery rhyme cards which can be enlarged, coloured and then laminated. Photocopiable pages 126 and 127 ('How well does it rhyme?' (1) and (2)) ask children to look closely at rhymes.

The record sheet on photocopiable page 128 focuses on children's growing knowledge of the relationship between the rhymes they hear and the patterns of letters in print.

'LUCKY DIP': A RHYMING GAME

For children to recognise that by changing the 'onset' (initial consonant phoneme) of a word that a new word can be created.

†† *Small group. In this example, four players.*
🕒 *15 minutes.*

Previous skills/knowledge needed
Children should have experience of listening and looking for words that rhyme within meaningful contexts, together with some previous knowledge of building rhyme families. They should have participated in activities where the terms 'rhyme', 'sound patterns', 'word families' or 'rhyme families' have been used. They may have recognised that by changing the 'onset' (the first consonant or cluster of consonants) it is possible to create a new word. Their experience will probably have been mainly with monosyllabic words.

Key background information

Children's phonemic awareness can be enhanced by plenty of experience of working with rhyme families. They require practice at substituting initial phonemes in order to discover that new words can be created. By focusing on words with 'onsets' (single consonants and clusters of consonants at the beginning of words) and 'rimes' (the following vowel and the remaining letters of the word) the teacher is able to help the children segment words in meaningful ways. This is beneficial to both spelling development as well as their reading. By working from the oral to the written form children are supported in their efforts to make links between what they can hear and what they can see.

Preparation

Prepare and label the 'Lucky Dip' container. This could be a bag or a small box, such as a shoebox. The four rhyme families targeted in this activity are 'at', 'en', 'un' and 'and', although you may wish to vary the selection according to the experience of the class. Four key words for the rhyme families might be 'cat', 'ten', 'sun' and 'sand'. Write each of these words on a card and place them in the 'Lucky Dip' container. Then copy photocopiable page 129 on to card, laminate it and cut out the individual cards to make four sets of 'picture clue' rhyme families. Finally, prepare and label the four rhyme family 'picture clue boxes' and place the 'picture clue' cards inside the appropriate box.

Resources needed

'Lucky Dip' container, key cards, picture clue cards and boxes (see 'Preparation'), flip chart, pens, alphabet frieze, blank cards.

What to do

Before starting the game place the rhyme family key cards in the 'Lucky Dip' container. Tell the children that they will be working with rhyming words. Check that everyone understands what a rhyming word is and provide examples if necessary. Explain to the children that they will take turns to pull one word out of the 'Lucky Dip' container. Demonstrate the rules by taking the first word out yourself. If, for example, the word is 'cat', read the card and place it face up on the table. Ask the child on your right to think of a word that rhymes with 'cat'. If the child makes a suitable response, such as 'hat', he then turns to the child on his right and says, 'Think of a word that rhymes with "hat".' The children should keep taking turns or say 'pass' if they cannot make a suggestion, until the round is exhausted. The last person to suggest a rhyme with 'cat' then restarts the game by taking a new 'Lucky Dip' card. If children have difficulty thinking of a word, ask them to choose a different letter of the alphabet and to try adding it to '–at', to see whether this would make a new word they recognise.

Suggestion(s) for extension

At the start of the game scribe the first word pulled from the 'Lucky Dip' on to the flip chart. As the children suggest additional rhymes add these to the list, encouraging the children to identify which sound has to be changed (ie. the onset) and which part of the word should remain constant (ie. the rime). Do this for all the 'Lucky Dip' families that are drawn from the tin. Encourage discussion about graphic similarities and differences. The children should also consider why certain suggestions were rejected. The words identified by the children for each rhyme family could then be written on to cards and illustrated.

Suggestion(s) for support

Children who find this activity difficult should first be encouraged to use oral skills to help them. Ask them to try to recall the words already suggested in the round to help them focus on the sound patterns. Sometimes, hearing a sequence of words will trigger the pattern to be continued. See if they can listen carefully to identify which part of the word changes and which stays the same. This is important for developing their sensitivity to rhyme. However, if a child still finds it difficult to participate then give him a clue, for example: 'You wear it on your head.' (Hat.)

Another way of supplying clues is to use the 'picture clue boxes' where all the possible rhymes for the activity have been written and illustrated on cards. The child could then be guided, for example, to the 'at' family box, select a card and then say the word. If the word has already been suggested then the child can select a further 'picture clue card' from the box.

Some children may find that working with decontextualised words is too challenging, in which case more experience of working with nursery rhymes might be useful. Alternatively, the 'Lucky Dip' activity could be shortened and simplified to one rhyme per day rather than playing with several rhymes.

Assessment opportunities

The emphasis in this activity is on the children's skills at listening to rhymes. Note who can add to rhyme families with ease and who cannot. Do children make suggestions systematically, such as running through the alphabet to change the initial sound? Are some children happy to suggest and then reject nonsense words? Some children will reveal spelling skills having understood that the substitution of the onset can produce a new word. Some children will suggest   onsets which consist only of single consonants, for example 't' or 'b', while others will confidently suggest words with initial consonant blends, such as 'st' or 'sp', or use consonant digraphs, such as 'ch' or 'sh'. These varying levels of response should be recorded and could form the basis of rhyme families for future games of 'Lucky Dip'.

Opportunities for IT

Children could extend this activity using a talking word process and a spelling checker. They could enter their 'new' rhyming word, check it using the speech option on the word processor and also check any unfamiliar words against the spelling dictionary to make sure the word is a real one rather than a nonsense word. If there is a thesaurus as well children could look at the meaning of any new words.

Picture clue cards

Display ideas

The 'Lucky Dip' container could be displayed with a different set of key words placed in it on a weekly or daily basis, and a notice inviting children to play such as 'Can you remember all the rhymes in these Rhyme families? Choose a friend and come and play this game.' This would provide the children with opportunities for independent practice. The appropriate set of 'picture clue cards' should also be available, as should the 'Rhyme Happy Family' cards if these have been made by the children.

Aspects of the English PoS covered

Speaking and listening – 1c; 2a.
Reading – 2b.

Reference to photocopiable sheet

The picture cards on photocopiable page 129 should be used as 'picture clues' in the support activity.

ODD ONE OUT (1)

To help children hear differences in sound patterns and rhyme and link these to letter patterns in print.
†† *Small group: 2–4 players.*
⏱ *15 minutes.*

Previous skills/knowledge needed

Children should have some experience of listening to and reciting rhymes and some familiarity with the terms 'rhyme' and 'pattern'. The children should have had their attention drawn to monosyllabic words and may recognise some words by sight.

Key background information

This activity is based on Bradley and Bryant's odd-one-out test (1983) in which they asked children to identify the odd-one-out in a set of four words which were selected either on the basis of their alliteration or rhyme. The children might be asked, for example, to listen to the following set of words: 'hen', 'pen', 'pig', 'men' and then be asked to identify the odd word out. It was found that children as young as four and five had the sensitivity to make these phonemic distinctions, but that this ability to distinguish the odd one out was weaker in a significant number of the older struggling readers in the study. This research demonstrates that success in the odd-one-out activity at four or five provides a

good predictor of later achievement in reading. This activity focuses mainly on rhyme and draws on both the child's ability to distinguish words by listening but also by utilising their graphic knowledge. However, the activity can be easily adapted to shift the focus to alliteration.

Preparation

Copy photocopiable pages 130 and 131 on to card. Laminate and cut out the cards to form two 'Odd One Out' packs of rhyme family cards. Prepare some more challenging 'Odd One Out' packs for the extension activity. Prepare one pack of alliterative 'Odd One Out' cards in the same way using photocopiable page 132.

Resources needed

Two packs of 'Odd One Out' rhyme family cards and one pack of alliterative 'Odd One Out' cards (see 'Preparation').

What to do

Begin the session by singing/reciting familiar rhymes, such as 'Humpty Dumpty' or 'One, two, buckle my shoe', and checking children's familiarity with rhyming words. Then introduce the 'Odd One Out' activity. First of all, play 'Odd One Out' orally by asking the children to listen to a set of words and identify the word that does not sound the same. Read out a set of words such as: 'man', 'can', 'fan', 'cup', 'ran'. What did they notice? Can they explain the similarities and differences that they heard? Repeat this part of the activity until most of the children show some evidence of phonological awareness.

Then move on to look at the words in their printed form. Select one of the packs of rhyme family cards, for example the 'at' family. Find a rhyming card, for example the 'cat' card, and retain it to use as a 'start' card at the beginning of the activity. Shuffle the rest of the cards and place them face down in the middle of the table. Explain to the children that they are going to work in two teams (pairs). Place the 'start' card on the table face up and then each pair takes turns to take the next card off the pile. They must see whether the card they pick up rhymes with the start card. If their card rhymes it should be placed face up on top of the start card. Explain to them that some cards have been deliberately placed in the pack which do not belong to the 'at' rhyme family and, if the children turn one of these up, they must call out 'odd one out' as quickly as possible. The rejected cards will be placed in a separate pile. Continue to play the game until all the cards are exhausted. At the end of the activity spread out the family of rhyming words so that the children can look at similarities and differences. Then look at the 'Odd One Out' cards and discuss why these had to be rejected. If the children responded well to the activity, select another pack of 'Odd One Out' cards and play a further game. This time the game could be played working with the alliterative words.

Suggestion(s) for extension

Children who cope easily with the activity should be asked to explain how they identified certain words as being the odd one out. These children should be able to identify significant differences both in the sound and spelling of the words. They should then move on to a more challenging pack of 'Odd One Out' cards.

Take the opportunity to discuss some of the inconsistencies in the English language by using the following set of words: 'book', 'hook', 'cook', 'tooth', 'look'. In this set the vowel digraph 'oo' is common to all the words but, in most regions of England, sounds slightly different in 'tooth'. The sound that 'oo' makes is dependent on regional accent and this can give rise to further discussion with the children.

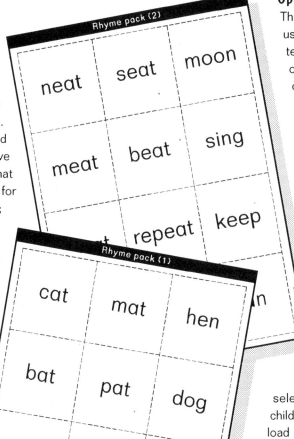

Suggestion(s) for support

Some children may find the opening, oral part of the activity difficult. These children should be given further opportunities to try to identify the odd one out from listening to sets of monosyllabic rhyming and alliterative words. Work with different rhyme and alliterative families using four or five words and include one word that sounds very obviously different: for instance, 'day', 'say', 'pig', 'way'; or 'cat', 'car', 'dog', 'cup'. Help the children to listen to the differences. If further use is made of the cards, reduce the number in the packs and include only one card that is the 'Odd One Out' (choose a word that sounds clearly different from the rhyme or alliterative family being used). At the beginning of the game, indicate to the children that there is just one word that does not belong to the set and that they must keep their ears and eyes open in order to spot it. Finally, to narrow the focus even further, it might be more appropriate to repeat sets of words worked with orally in the written form of the activity.

Assessment opportunities

The children will reveal by their oral contributions their current ability to identify words that do/do not rhyme. In the card game they will/will not successfully identify 'Odd One Out' cards by drawing on their graphic knowledge as well as what they can hear. Some children will go on to make fresh rhyme families with the 'Odd One Out' cards and may be able to do so independently. Children will/will not comment on changing onsets and the constancy of the rimes. Children's growing ability to recognise words out of context can also be assessed through this activity.

Opportunities for IT

The activity could be extended by using a talking word processor. The teacher could prepare some families of words which include an odd one out. The children could listen to each word read by the word processor to help them decide which is the odd one out. This word could be deleted from the list, leaving only the rhyming words. The final list could be printed out for assessment purposes. It would be possible to prepare several different lists at differing levels to cater for a range of abilities.

In order to undertake this activity children will need to know how to move the cursor around the screen to the set of words, use the speech facility and delete the selected word. Older or more able children could also be shown how to load the prepared list of words into the word processor to begin the activity and to print out their completed and revised list.

Display ideas

The 'Odd One Out' packs can be displayed on a table, along with some of the objects named, and made available for children to work with independently.

Aspects of the English PoS covered

Speaking and listening – 3a.
Reading – 2d.
Writing – 2d.

Reference to photocopiable sheets

Photocopiable pages 130 and 131 contain two sets of 'Odd One Out' rhyme packs. Each of these consists of eight rhyming words and four rogue words. Photocopiable page 132 contains a set of eight alliterative words and four rogue words.

ODD ONE OUT (2)

To help children hear differences in sound patterns and rhyme and link these to patterns in print.

†† *Small group: a game for four players (or eight if they play in pairs).*

🕐 *20 minutes.*

Previous skills/knowledge needed
Children should have experience of listening to rhymes and reciting them and be familiar with the terms 'rhyme' and 'pattern' when talking about rhymes. They should be used to listening to and discussing monosyllabic words that rhyme.

Key background information
Young children's ability to hear the odd word out from a set of rhyming or alliterative words has been shown to be an important factor in later success in reading. Encouraging children to talk about the similarities between the rhyming words and to consider their reasons for identifying a word as being an odd one out will help them think about words analytically and apply their knowledge when they look at the same words in print.

Shuffle the remaining rhyme family cards, along with the four rogue cards and place them in the 'Odd One Out' box.

Resources needed
'Odd One Out' box and a set of rhyme family cards (see 'Preparation'), blank cards, pens.

What to do
Start the session by reciting/singing a well-loved nursery rhyme and discuss the rhymes and alliterative sounds that the children can hear. Check that the children understand what is meant by the term 'rhyming words'.

Introduce the odd-one-out idea by asking the children to listen to a set of four words which should rhyme. They must listen carefully in case one of the words does not belong to the set. Recite four monosyllabic words, for example 'cat', 'hat', 'dog', 'bat'. Ask the children to identify the words that rhymed or that had the same sound pattern. If they do not volunteer the information ask, 'Which word was the odd one out and didn't rhyme?' The children should agree on 'dog'. Repeat this part of the activity with different rhymes so that the children become familiar with the idea of listening for the 'odd one out'.

Preparation
Decorate a shoebox and label it 'Odd One Out'. This will be the container for the playing cards. Copy photocopiable page 133 or 134 on to card, laminate it and cut out the individual cards. The words on photocopiable page 133 are more suitable for beginners. Use four blank cards as 'rogue' cards. Write on these cards four words unrelated to the rhyme families which are being focused on in the session. Before starting the game take one card from each of the different rhyme families (these will be used to determine which rhyme each of the four players will be collecting during the game).

Once children have had plenty of experience listening for the 'odd one out' tell them that they are going to collect sets of four words which all belong to the same rhyme family. Each child takes one of the four cards held by the teacher (see 'Preparation'). The card they choose determines the rhyme family they will be collecting. Each child should place her card face up on the table in front of her. Tell the children that each set contains four cards. As they all have the first card in their set, they now have three more cards to collect. However, there are also four 'rogue' cards to look out for which do not belong to any of the rhyme families.

SPELLING AND
PHONICS KS1

The game proceeds with the children taking turns to select a card from the 'Odd One Out' box, starting with the player sitting on the right of the teacher. The first child should identify her rhyme family by reading the card which she selected at the start of the game. She should then take a card out of the 'Odd One Out' box, read it and decide whether it fits her particular rhyme family. If the card belongs to her rhyme family, she should keep it and select another from the box. If the card does not belong she should say 'Odd one out' and offer it to the other members of the group. If another player can use the card it should be handed over to them. Play then moves to the child sitting on the right of the first child.

If a child selects one of the four 'rogue' cards, the card should be placed face up in the middle of the table. Play then moves to the player sitting on the child's right. The main part of the game concludes when all the cards have found a home. (The 'rogue' cards will be used in the extension activity.)

Suggestion(s) for extension
Ask the children to justify why they judge a card to belong to their rhyme family or not. If they select a 'rogue' card, they should explain why it cannot belong to any of the rhyme families.

Ask each child to select one of the 'rogue' cards and to think of three words to complete its rhyme family. They should write these on blank playing cards, thinking carefully about the spelling. The 'rogue' card will support them in their spelling as they think about the letter patterns.

The children could then return to the teacher's demonstration of the 'odd one out' idea at the start of the session. They can work in pairs to suggest four words for the other children to listen to in order to spot the 'odd one out'.

These children could then go on to make a fresh 'Odd One Out' game based on alliterative words.

Suggestion(s) for support
Some children may not be able to proceed beyond the first part of the session. They should be given plenty of opportunities to repeat the opening activity and could take turns round the group to think of more sets of words that rhyme. For each set they work with, the children could then take turns to suggest one extra word that they think would be an odd word out.

When working with these children in the main activity, the 'rogue' cards could be removed from the pack so that the children are able to focus on completing the four rhyme families. The rhyme family cards could be illustrated to support the printed word. Alternatively, in order to give them more support, they could work in paired teams on a rhyme family. With some children it might be more suitable if the teacher handled the complete pack of cards herself, turning the words up and discussing them. The children could be asked to help her decide which words rhyme and which words are 'odd ones out'. The whole group could help in constructing the four rhyming families.

Assessment opportunities
From this activity it will be possible to identify children who can hear words that do/do not belong to a particular rhyme family. It will also be possible to see how children apply this knowledge visually when they look at cards and make decisions as to which rhyme family they belong to and why. With the 'rogue' cards they will demonstrate their ability to create new rhyme families and apply their knowledge of the rhyme patterns in the spelling of the words. Children who make the alliterative game suggested as an extension activity will show their sensitivity to alliteration.

Display ideas
The 'Odd One Out' box and the pack of rhyme cards can be placed on a small table for future games. If the alliterative set is made, this too can be made available to the children. Notices inviting the children to come and play the 'Odd One Out' game should be displayed alongside.

Aspects of the English PoS covered
Reading – 2b.
Writing – 2d.

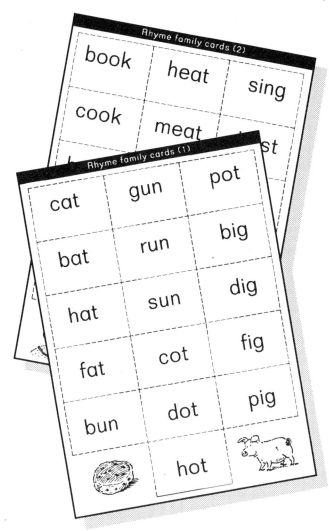

Key background information

Research into children's early phonemic awareness has shown that awareness of rhyme is a crucial factor in children's later literacy development. It is important to sustain, develop and heighten this phonological awareness in the classroom. In writing a rhyming poem children will inevitably encounter rhymes which are spelled differently, which will promote discussion of letter strings.

Preparation

Make a large-format version of the rhyme 'One, two, buckle my shoe'. This can be taken from photocopiable page 123 if you wish. Mount it on card, colour it and laminate it.

Resources needed

Enlarged poetry card of 'One, two, buckle my shoe', flip chart, pens, paper.

What to do

Start the session off by everyone reciting some favourite rhymes and poems (select rhymes with rhyming couplets) concluding with 'One, two, buckle my shoe'. Use the enlarged

Reference to photocopiable sheets

Photocopiable pages 133 and 132 each provide words from four rhyme families to be made into playing cards. The set on photocopiable page 133 may be better suited to beginners. One word from each of the four families on the page that is not being used can be taken to make the 'rogue' cards.

THE OPPOSITES RHYME

To help children apply their oral knowledge of rhyme to the written forms of rhyming words.

†† *Small group or whole class activity.*

⏲ *30–40 minutes.*

Previous skills/knowledge needed

Children will need experience of listening to, reciting and learning nursery rhymes and poems. They should also know how to listen out for and identify rhymes when joining in with nursery rhymes and poems. They should have some experience of composing rhymes/poems in a whole group setting. Some experience of talking about opposites and compiling pairs of opposites will also be useful.

poetry card as an example to discuss the rhyme pattern and see if the children can suggest some other pairs of rhymes that follow similar patterns, for example 'four/floor' or 'bear/chair'. On the flip chart list pairs of rhymes identified by the children. As these are listed encourage children's comments and observations about the similarities and differences in the pairs of rhymes – this might include differences in spellings/letter strings.

Next, explain that they will be working as a group to compose an 'Opposites Rhyme'. Collect from the children some examples of opposites and list them separately on the flip chart. (These examples will provide a useful 'ideas bank' to refer back to as the activity progresses.) At this point remind the group of the two essential components of this

rhyme, that is rhyming pairs of words which come at the end of lines and pairs of opposites. In order to clarify the task provide a brief example along the lines of:

Our Opposites Rhyme
As big as a house,
as small as a mouse,
as high as a tree,
as low as my knee,
as happy as Jim,
as sad as Tim, etc.

The example above could be used as a 'starter' to set the pattern of the poem.

As the children compose fresh lines, these should be scribed on the flip chart by the teacher. Conduct this as a shared writing activity and encourage the children to discuss similarities and differences in the graphic representation of the rhymes and hypothesise on how words should be spelled. When everyone has offered a contribution, conclude the rhyme and read it through together. Afterwards, focus on the rhymes and ask the children to read them as quickly as possible, from the first to the last and back up again. This will promote speedy word recognition of words with familiar patterns.

In a later session, pairs of children could act out the rhyme or it could be used in PE as part of a movement lesson.

Suggestion(s) for extension
Having participated in composing the first few couplets of the main activity, some children could then work individually or in pairs to produce their own rhymes. As the children work on the poem ask them how they make decisions about the spelling of some of the pairs of rhymes. Once completed, their versions could be read aloud at the end of the session and compared to the main group's rhyme.

Suggestion(s) for support
With a small group of children it is possible to take a highly structured approach. List a small number of opposites, for example 'big' and 'little', on the flip chart. Then help them to think of an equal number of pairs of rhymes. Use either known rhymes or poems as a source of ideas or, if this is not successful, simply suggest a word, for example 'men', and ask the children to think of a rhyme to go with it, for example 'ten'. Then, using the above formula for the structure of the poem, take the first opposite on the list and the first rhyme and compose the first two lines. For example:

As big as men,
as little as ten...

Then involve the children, asking them to help select the next items on the list. Draw their attention to the changes that occur in the initial letter of the second rhyming word of each pair.

Assessment opportunities
By requiring them to think of pairs of rhymes this activity enables the children's knowledge of rhyme to be assessed. It also provides information about their growing awareness of the graphic similarities and differences of rhyming words. Careful questioning during the shared writing activity will reveal the children's ability to spell rhyming words, that is by

changing the 'onset' – the beginning consonant or consonant cluster. The children's confidence in reading rhyming words and the strategies used to decode them can also be observed. By asking them to read the rhyming words as quickly as possible you can assess their developing sight vocabulary.

Opportunities for IT
Children could use a word processor to produce their own rhyming poems. They could use a talking word processor to check their rhymes as they write them or when the poem is completed. They might also be shown how to use a spelling checker to check the spellings of their new rhymes. The completed poem could be printed out for display purposes.

Display ideas
The shared writing poem can be illustrated and displayed as a poetry card. Children's individual rhymes could be word processed and compiled into a book.

Aspects of the English PoS covered
Reading – 2b.

ALLITERATIVE NAME BOOK

To develop alphabetic knowledge and sensitivity to alliteration.

†† *Whole class, then individuals.*

🕐 *Approximately 20 minutes with the whole class; 20 minutes individual work; 10-15 minutes to read the book and conclude the activity.*

Previous skills/knowledge needed
Children should know their own names and be familiar with the sound of the first letter of their name. The class should be familiar with a range of ABC books including some that emphasise alliteration, for example Martin Leman and Angela Carter's *Comic and Curious Cats* (1990, Gollancz). They should have made links between the first letter of their own names and the appropriate pages in the ABC books they have met. They will have to have discussed letter order, whose name comes higher up or lower down in the alphabet, and they should have noticed that other words start with the same sound as their own name.

Key background information
Children's ability to hear alliteration, sound patterns and rhyme, has been shown to be a key factor in their ability to benefit from instruction in phonics. It is important to develop their auditory abilities and awareness of sounds as a first step into reading.

Preparation
Ensure that all children are familiar with the idea of an ABC book. Prepare a 'big book' with a page for every child in the class. Write each child's initial letter at the top of a piece of paper and display a list of the class's names on the flip chart to refer to when necessary.

Resources needed
A prepared blank 'big book', a page for each child with his initial letter printed on it, a list of the children's names displayed prominently, pencils, coloured pencils or crayons, adhesive.

What to do
Explain to the class that they will be helping you to make a class Name Book with a difference. Remind them of an alliterative ABC book (such as *Comic and Curious Cats*) which they have heard before. If you have a copy in the classroom, read it through with them. Tell them that their ABC book will be amusing and will be all about what they can do. Take each child's name in turn and start off with some examples, such as 'Anthony acts', 'Baljit boxes', 'Charlie chatters' and so on. Ask the children if they notice anything special about the examples. Focus on the initial sounds of the words to illustrate the alliterative nature of the pairs of words. Discuss the remaining names and ensure that everyone has a suitable alliterative word to go with their name. Children may suggest pairs of words that are alliterative but reveal inconsistencies, for example 'Philip flies'. These will provide opportunities for discussion later on.

Then ask the children to write their pairs of words on the paper provided and to think carefully about how to illustrate their action, for example 'Simon smiles'. As they complete the task ask them to find the correct page in the ABC book and stick their work in. Each child should illustrate their own name.

To conclude, give the book a title and read it through with the class while individual children perform the actions to accompany their particular entry.

Suggestion(s) for extension

Children could take a set of, say, six names in the class and write and illustrate their own alliterative book about them. The same idea could be repeated using animals, for example 'alligators argue'. Children could perform their actions while others in the class read the text aloud. The book could be put on tape and used in the listening corner. A rhyming alliterative poem would be a further development of the activity.

Suggestion(s) for support

The whole activity could be carried out through shared writing, ie. with the teacher scribing straight into the prepared 'big book' as the children offer their ideas. The children could then draw pictures of themselves carrying out the actions which match their names and these could then be pasted in the book. If the actions chosen by the children are too difficult for them to draw, then photographs of the children carrying out or miming the actions could be taken and used to illustrate the book.

In a class where individual children are having difficulty, ask them to try to write the letters of their names that they know and the first letter of the alliterative word and then scribe for them, commenting on the sounds and letters. Some children may wish to copy or trace over their pair of words.

Assessment opportunities

Note who can/cannot think of an alliterative word for their name. Observe children who readily offer suggestions for other names in the class besides their own. Where appropriate, encourage children to comment on inconsistencies in the initial letter used to represent their own or other children's pair of words, for example 'Philip flies'. On subsequent re-readings look for children who widen their repertoire by responding to other people's pages in the book as well as their own.

Opportunities for IT

The children could use a word processor or simple desk top publishing package to produce their own alliterative name book. A class book could be set up in advance by the teacher with a page for each child to type in their alliterative name. Illustrations could be added by hand after the page has been printed.

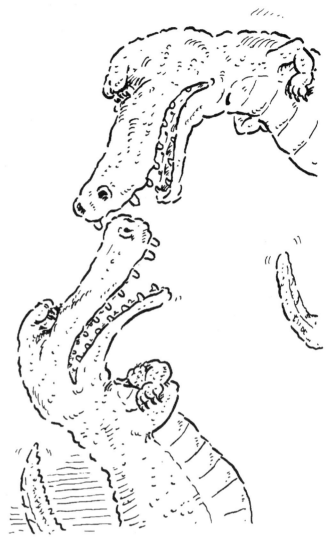

An alternative approach would be to use an art or drawing package so that the children could use the text facilities to type in their alliterative name and then the drawing facilities to illustrate their page. If the drawing is done on the computer the activity will need to be spread across several days to ensure that children have time to experiment and explore the drawing package, particularly if they have not used one before. They will need to be shown how to enter their text and position it on the page, how to create simple shapes, stretch and size them, move them to new positions, alter the line thickness and change and fill their shapes with colour. Ideally children should have access to a colour printer to make their final printouts. The completed book could be bound for future reading by the class.

Display ideas

The completed 'big book' could be placed in the book corner for shared reading sessions. An alternative format could be to make a zigzag book which will stand up on a flat surface.

Aspects of the English PoS covered

Reading – 2b.

TERRIFIC TONGUE TWISTERS

To provide children with experience and a heightened awareness of alliteration through hearing and reciting tongue twisters.

†† *Small or large group.*

⏲ *15 minutes.*

Previous skills/knowledge needed

The children may already have encountered alliteration through previous experience of rhymes, jingles and songs. They may have commented that some words in rhymes and phrases in stories start with the same sound. They may also have noticed that sounds recur within words.

Key background information

Children who have had experience of listening for, discussing and identifying initial sounds in words will be able to apply this knowledge when discussing the tongue twisters. Equally, children who lack this experience will find this activity helps them to increase their sensitivity to alliteration and to the initial and recurring sounds in words. Teachers need to know which children need to develop their awareness in this respect, as it appears to be essential in early reading development.

Resources needed

A collection of tongue twisters and alliterative nursery rhymes.

What to do

Recite the following rhyme to the children:

Peter Piper picked a peck of pickled pepper.
If Peter Piper picked a peck of pickled pepper,
Where's the peck of pickled pepper
Peter Piper picked?

Tell them that this is a very special kind of rhyme called a 'tongue twister'. The first time they hear the rhyme they should listen but next time through they can all join in together.

Having recited the tongue twister together, ask them to practise saying it in pairs, then gather their reactions – for example, whether they found it amusing and why, or if they found that they tripped up over certain words. The children should comment on the abundance of words that start with the same sound (or have the sound occurring in them more than once) and should be asked to try to identify the sound, how many times they can hear it and in which words.

To conclude, recite the tongue twister at speed and then as slowly as possible. If appropriate, repeat the activity using a different tongue twister, for example 'Betty Botter':

Betty Botter bought some butter
But the butter Berry bought was bitter,
So Betty Botter bought some better butter
Better than the bitter butter
Betty bought before.

Suggestion(s) for extension

The children could try substituting some of the key words in one of the tongue twisters with ideas of their own, for example: 'Peter Piper packed a pot of peppermint pears.'

SPELLING AND PHONICS KS1

Having worked with tongue twisters that focus on initial single consonants the children can try tongue twisters that use consonant digraphs, such as 'She sells sea shells on the sea shore.' If this tongue twister is recited at speed the children will discover that they make amusing mistakes that change the meaning, for example: 'Sea shells she sells on the she saw.' This could then open up opportunities for discussion about which elements of the words changed in order to alter the meaning.

Suggestion(s) for support

Children who found the main activity difficult should be encouraged to say the first few lines of one of the tongue twisters slowly and rhythmically, emphasising the alliterative sound. This may require demonstration, for example: 'Peter Piper picked a peck of pickled peppers.' Ask if they can hear the 'p' sound. How many times can they hear it? Encourage them to count on their fingers or tap as they hear the sound. These children may feel more confident if they work with familiar nursery rhymes, such as 'Sing a song of sixpence'.

Assessment opportunities

The level of the children's involvement in the main activity can be gauged by whether they joined in with the tongue twister or did so intermittently. Some children may choose to listen. Ask the children to explain what they notice about the tongue twisters, that is repeated use of the same initial or similar sounds. Note whether children can successfully identify the sound and indicate the frequency with which it is used (a variety of strategies may be used to achieve this including tapping or counting). The child's ability to substitute words to create a variation on the original tongue twister will not only indicate sensitivity to alliteration but also an understanding of its function in language. Some children may demonstrate this knowledge more confidently through the use of an alliterative nursery rhyme.

Opportunities for IT

Children could use a word processor with a prepared tongue twister file. The tongue twister file could be loaded into the word processor and children experiment by editing it to substitute new words to fit the tongue twister. It is important

that they do not delete all of the text back to the word they wish to change and they will need to be shown how to move the cursor around the screen to the words to be altered, make deletions and insertions into the text. The final version could be saved and printed out for display purposes.

Children might also use the speech facility of a talking word processor to listen to the tongue twister. Some children may notice that although they can speed up the speech it does not copy the rhythm of the tongue twister. This would be a good time to discuss some of the limitations of the speech facility.

Display ideas

The tongue twister could be displayed in its written form with illustrations to accompany it. A tongue twister cassette could also be made.

Aspects of the English PoS covered

Reading – 2b.

CREATING TONGUE TWISTERS

To further develop children's knowledge of alliteration through reading and writing tongue twisters.
†† *Small or large group.*
🕑 *40 minutes.*

Previous skills/knowledge needed

Childen should have experience of discussing initial and recurring sounds in words and some may have gained experience of utilising their implicit knowledge of alliteration by composing alternative versions of tongue twisters. All children need to have experience of playing with language and noticing the resulting effects, for example the creation of nonsense words or subtle changes in meaning.

Key background information

Children play with language from a very early age and teachers need to capitalise on their enjoyment of this activity. By reflecting on their play children can be helped to make their implicit knowledge explicit.

Preparation

Make poetry cards of familiar tongue twisters and alliterative nursery rhymes by copying and enlarging photocopiable pages 135 and 136 on to (minimum) A3-size card. These can be illustrated either by sticking on appropriate cut-out drawings or by drawing directly on to the card. The cards should be laminated to increase their durability.

Resources needed

Tongue twister cards (see 'Preparation'), flip chart, stand, pointer, pens, drawing materials, cassette player and blank cassette.

What to do

To introduce the session check children's previous experience of tongue twisters. Identify and focus on the children's favourite tongue twister, placing, if possible, the appropriate tongue twister card on the flip chart stand. Ask the children to read the tongue twister aloud and point to the words as they read. Afterwards, draw their attention to the poem and ask them to comment on anything that they notice about the words. The children should recognise that the same initial sound is used to start the alliterative words.

Unless children have already had experience of doing so, they should now compose their own collaborative, alternative version of, say, 'Peter Piper'. Display the 'Peter Piper' card in a prominent place to use as a reference and then, using the flip chart, scribe the alternative version for them. The children should decide on the choice of words and their spellings, paying particular attention to the initial sounds of the alliterative words. They may move away completely from the original structure of the tongue twister or they could be guided to follow the structure more closely by noticing which words recur, in order to complete the idea.

Read the new version through with the children and allow them to make any alterations and additions. The children should not only notice the recurring letters in alliterative language but also the potential for word play and nonsense.

To conclude, the children can record their new tongue twister and illustrate it.

Suggestion(s) for extension

Having written an alternative version with the whole group, children could pair up and write another alternative or a variation on one of the other tongue twisters or nursery rhymes.

Suggestion(s) for support

For children who found the main activity difficult, working with a short, well-known nursery rhyme might be more effective, for example 'Sing a song of sixpence'. Talk about the first line, drawing attention to the initial sound 's', and ask the children if they can think of a word beginning with 's' that could replace 'sixpence'. Give them an example, such

as 'Sing a song of saucepans'. Can the children think of another variation? Then pick up on the next strongly alliterative line: 'Four and twenty blackbirds baked in a pie'. Identify the key alliterative pattern (the 'b' sound) and discuss the words. Keep most of the line intact but ask the children to think of a word starting with 'b' that could replace 'pie'. Give them an example to help them, such as 'Four and twenty blackbirds baked in a bean'. Finally, scribe their variation of the rhyme on the flip chart.

Assessment opportunities

Observe the children's ability to connect the alliterations they hear with the patterns in print when they read and comment on the tongue twister cards. Leading questions, such as 'What do you notice about many of the words?' may be needed to prompt an appropriate response. As they compose alternative versions, the children's awareness of alliteration

will be revealed when they help identify the words that they might want to change and also in the words that they suggest. Some children may suggest words that do not quite fit the alliterative pattern, such as 'Percy *Banana* packed...' The children should be encouraged to debate whether the word 'banana' is a close enough fit to the alliterative pattern. Some children may suggest a word that fits alliteratively but has a different initial letter, eg. 'f' and 'ph'. This in itself could present an opportunity to look more closely at the reasons why 'f' and 'ph' represent the same sound.

SPELLING AND
PHONICS KS1

Opportunities for IT

Children could work in small groups to write their tongue twister using a word processor or simple desk top publishing package. They should be given time to originate their work on the computer rather than typing in handwritten work. This activity will give children opportunities to draft and redraft their work, possibly making printed copies to work on away from the computer and returning to retrieve and edit their file. This would give children opportunities to save and retrieve their work.

Children might also use the facilities of a talking word processor to listen to their developing tongue twister, or be shown how to use the spelling checker to ensure that all of their spellings are correct. They could also be introduced to an electronic thesaurus, either on the computer or a hand held version to think of new or different words to fit into their tongue twister.

Display ideas

The newly composed tongue twisters can be illustrated and displayed on the wall. They can also be recorded on cassette for future listening.

Aspects of the English PoS covered

Speaking and listening – 1a; 3b.
Reading – 2b.

Reference to photocopiable sheets

Photocopiable pages 135 and 136 provide four popular tongue twisters, which should each be enlarged to a minimum of A3 size, for work with the class.

Betty Botter

Betty Botter bought some butter
But the butter Betty bought was bitter.
So Betty Botter bought some better butter,
Better than the bitter butter
Betty bought before.

Peter Piper

Peter Piper picked a peck of pickled pepper.
If Peter Piper picked a peck of pickled pepper,
Where's the peck of pickled pepper
Peter Piper picked?

She sells sea shells

She sells sea shells
By the sea shore.
The shells that she sells
Are sea shells, I'm sure.

SPELLING AND
PHONICS KS1

CRAZY, TONGUE TWISTING, NONSENSE SENTENCES

To consolidate children's knowledge of alliteration by focusing on the written patterns in alliterative sentences.

†† *Small or large group. Starting with the whole group, moving into pair work.*

⏲ *30–45 minutes.*

Previous skills/knowledge needed

Children will need experience of alliteration through rhymes, jingles, songs and tongue twisters. (They may have participated in the previous two activities 'Terrific tongue twisters' and 'Creating tongue twisters'.) They should have a knowledge of tongue twisters and have noticed the significance of initial and recurring sounds in alliterative words. Through shared reading and writing activities they may also have recognised that alliterative words can have similar sounds but use different letters to represent those sounds, for example 'f' and 'ph'.

Key background information

Playing with language and the creation of nonsense words and phrases will have been a part of the children's experience from their very earliest years and their enjoyment of this should be capitalised on in the classroom. Language play provides a very positive context for developing children's knowledge of the sounds of language and the ways these can be represented in writing.

Preparation

None specific to this activity, although poem, tongue twister and nursery rhyme cards could be made, if not already prepared for other activities (see 'Preparation' for the previous activity 'Creating tongue twisters'). Write the children's names on the flip chart and check the list to see whether anyone has an alliterative first name and surname.

Resources needed

List of class names on flip chart, selection of tongue twisters and rhymes on cards, picture dictionaries, paper, writing materials.

What to do

To introduce the activity recite some favourite tongue twisters and alliterative rhymes. If you have already done the previous activity 'Creating tongue twisters' the children may have composed some suitable examples. Using an enlarged version of one of the rhymes discuss the alliterative patterns and how these are achieved in written language. Explain to the children that the purpose of the activity will be to compose alliterative nonsense sentences. In order to write their alliterative sentences the children need to do two things: first, they must think up some alliterative names and surnames/family names (these terms may require explanation); secondly, they will need to think up lots of words that start with, or contain, the same sound. Some of these words may be nonsense words, for example 'bim', 'bam', 'bom'.

Start with an example, either using a name from the class list or by choosing a sound, such as 'm'. Then ask the group to help think up two pairs of first names and surnames, for example 'Mickey Mop' and 'Molly Mop'. Start off the alliterative sentence using the two pairs of names and ask the children to help compose the rest of the sentence. The following example gives an idea of the possibilities of the activity:

Mickey Mop and Molly Mop made marvellous, munchy, minty marmalade mousse.

After responding to the children's comments and questions, pair the children up and ask them to see if they can *each* think of an alliterative name and surname. They may want to use their own names, famous names or invent new ones. Before starting they should agree on the sound that they want to work with. Ask each pair to report back, first on their sound and then on their alliterative names. These can be written up on the flip chart. If necessary, use one of the examples given by the children as a basis for composing a further demonstration sentence with the whole group.

SPELLING AND
PHONICS KS1

Philip the flying phantom.

Then ask each pair to compose as long a sentence as possible starting with the alliterative names that they created. They should try spelling the words they use. Encourage the use of word play and nonsense words to help them sustain their ideas. When they have completed their sentences ask each pair to read their sentence to the class and to explain some of the decisions that they have made about the spelling of the alliterative words. It will be particularly interesting to discuss the spelling patterns of any nonsense words that have been created.

Suggestion(s) for extension

If the children have created lots of nonsense words, ask them to try to explain the meaning of their sentence. Challenge them to see who can write the longest alliterative sentence. Some may want to write additional sentences using the same sound or focusing on different sounds.

Suggestion(s) for support

Before writing their sentence down it may help the children to rehearse their ideas orally. Working with their partner they could take turns to suggest the next word or phrase in the sentence. Some children may be more successful if they work collaboratively in a group with the teacher scribing for them. Working with a chosen sound, list words suggested by the children on the flip chart and involve the children in deciding their suitability for the sentence.

Assessment opportunities

Observe how successfully children can compose alliterative sentences either orally or in writing. Some will try hard to include only words that are alliterative, while others will use fewer alliterative words or words that do not quite fit the alliterative pattern. Some children will comment on using words that sound similar but vary in their spelling patterns, for example 'ph' and 'f'. Children's hypotheses about the spelling patterns of the words can also be observed as they are encouraged to explain the logic behind the spelling of any nonsense words. They could also be asked to explain how successfully they think they have used their chosen alliterative sound, for example by reading their work through and indicating where the sound has occurred in different words.

Opportunities for IT

Children could use a word processor to create their nonsense sentences. This is an ideal activity as the amount of keyboarding is minimal, but as the work develops and children add new words to their sentence they will need to move the cursor around the screen, make insertions and deletions and gradually refine their sentence. Children could also be introduced to the features of the spelling checker to check their completed version, or to help them look for new words fitting in with their alliterative letter. When they have completed the sentence children can experiment with different fonts and sizes to prepare their work for printing out and display in the classroom.

Display ideas

The sentences can be illustrated and displayed on the wall or put into a book.

Aspects of the English PoS covered

Speaking and listening – 1a; 3b.
Reading – 2b.

Syllables

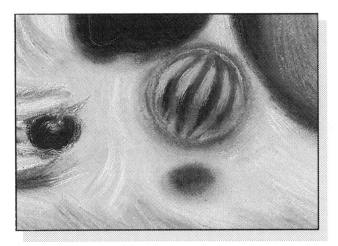

Children are born with a natural sensitivity to rhythm clearly demonstrated through their enthusiasm for physical activities such as jumping, bouncing, skipping and dancing. They also enjoy songs with strong rhythmic patterns and action rhymes. Children's love of rhythm provides an important link as they become aware of and develop their insights about syllables. Syllables provide the rhythm of words and are therefore essential building blocks of words.

A rule of thumb when trying to identify a syllable is that it should have a central vowel or diphthong which may be preceded by 0–3 consonants or followed by 0–4 consonants. Although many words follow one or other of these combinations, there are inevitably, exceptions.

It can be helpful when analysing syllables to think in terms of 'onsets' and 'rimes'. Peter Bryant and Usha Goswami's research in 1985 revealed that children as young as three had a sensitivity to 'onset' and 'rime'. Their later research (1990) has shown that children who were starting to read were able to use this natural sensitivity to 'chunk' words in meaningful ways.

Marie Clay (1993) recognises that, initially, children find it easier to hear bigger chunks in words than individual sounds. The first activities in this chapter encourage children to clap parts (syllables) of words that they can hear and to recognise patterns in words. Later activities shift the emphasis to the printed word, asking the children to look at similarities and differences, while the final activities ask children to apply their syllable knowledge in writing.

71

$\mathcal{S}$yllables

CLAPPING RHYMES

To provide children with experience of hearing rhythm within familiar rhymes. To recognise similarities and differences in rhythms through clapping.

†† *Whole class or small group.*

🕐 *40 minutes. Main activity 20 minutes; small group activities 20 minutes.*

Previous skills/knowledge needed
Children should have experience of joining in a wide range of clapping games, such as playground skipping games, football chants, action rhymes and nursery rhymes.

Key background information
Children have an implicit knowledge of rhythm which is demonstrated in a wide range of activities, including their love of rhyme. Children are drawn to nursery rhymes not only because of their rhyming and alliterative qualities but also due to the predictable and repetitive syllabic patterns which make many of these rhymes so memorable. Through the careful selection of nursery rhymes it is possible to provide children with clear contrasts between mono-and polysyllabic patterns.

Preparation
Photocopy and enlarge the nursery rhymes on photocopiable page 137. Laminate them to make large poetry cards. Record the rhymes on a cassette. Copy photocopiable pages 138 and 139.

Resources needed
Poetry cards (see 'Preparation'), writing and art materials, photocopiable pages 138 and 139, nursery rhyme cassette (see 'Preparation'), cassette player.

What to do
Sing through the nursery rhyme 'Jack and Jill' with the children. Then repeat it, asking the children to clap as they sing. They should try to clap on each segment of the words as they hear them. Then ask the children to say the rhyme through, clapping as they go. Speak the words rhythmically so that they can hear the patterns.

Next, split the group into two halves called 'A' and 'B'. Ask group 'A' to recite and clap the first half of the song and then ask group 'B' to complete it. Ask the children to listen to each group's rhythm and comment on what they hear. They may notice, for example, that the two halves of the song are rhythmically very similar. They may comment that the rhythm sounds a bit 'clip-cloppish' rather like horses' hooves. Can they clap the bits of the rhyme that sound like this? Draw attention to the polysyllabic words 'water' and 'tumbling' and contrast them with monosyllabic words, such as 'Jack' or 'crown'. Encourage children to clap these words and see if they notice differences.

Now repeat the activity with the second rhyme, 'Ten fat sausages'. As a contrast to 'Jack and Jill', this contains a large number of polysyllabic words.

Suggestion(s) for extension
Children who in the first rhyme are able to hear differences between monosyllabic and polysyllabic words can be asked to listen out for words that have different rhythms in the second rhyme. Which word do they think has the most claps and why? They could then work with the poetry cards and point to where they think the breaks come in the words. They can then go on to complete photocopiable pages 138 and 139.

Suggestion(s) for support
Some children will detect rhythm more effectively if they recite or sing the rhyme slowly, exaggerating all the parts of the words that they can hear. They may find that tapping the rhythm is more helpful than clapping it. Follow up the main activity by using the poetry cards with a small group, drawing attention to the long words which have lots of claps and the short words which have fewer claps. If the children do not know the rhymes off by heart, encourage them to return to them at regular intervals (see display idea using cassette player).

Assessment opportunities
Children's awareness of rhythm in words will be demonstrated by the accuracy with which they clap the patterns of the songs. Some children will do this more successfully if they

recite the rhyme slowly. The children's awareness of similarities and differences in individual words will also provide evidence of their knowledge of syllables. Some children will be able to identify the longest word(s) in each rhyme by counting the syllables and may make this knowledge explicit by examining the printed form of the word on the poetry cards or by their notation on the photocopiable sheet.

Display ideas
The children could decorate the poetry cards, which could then be displayed with the nursery rhyme cassette and cassette player for independent listening.

Aspects of the English PoS covered
Speaking and listening – 1a; 2b.
Reading – 2b.

Reference to photocopiable sheet
The two nursery rhymes used in this activity are provided on photocopiable page 137. These should be copied and enlarged to be made into individual poetry cards.

Photocopiable pages 138 and 139 ask the children to count the number of syllables (claps) in particular words in these rhymes.

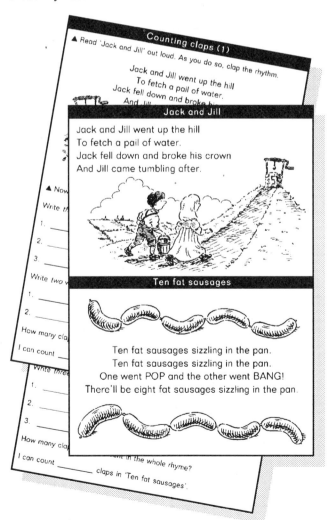

THE CLAPPING GAME

To help children listen for and identify syllables in individual words.

†† *Whole class or small group.*

⏲ *25 minutes. Introduction and main activity 15 minutes; extension and support activities 10 minutes.*

Previous skills/knowledge needed
Children should have experience of playing a variety of clapping games, including clapping as an accompaniment to favourite nursery rhymes and songs. Experience of rhythm may also have been gained through playing percussion instruments in music lessons.

Key background information
Children enjoy and actively respond to rhythm. By encouraging them to listen for syllables in words they will begin to recognise that words can be broken down into smaller units. Young children find it easier to identify the required number of syllables in a word than to tap out individual phonemes.

Resources needed
Cassette player and blank cassette.

What to do
Start by reciting several clapping rhymes or songs, such as 'Jack and Jill', with the children. Talk about the rhythm and encourage the children's comments. They may say 'some of it's jumpy', 'some of it's the same' or 'some of it's longer' and so on.

Syllables

Explain that in this session they are going to think about the rhythm that they can hear in individual words and that they will start by listening to the rhythm of their own names. Give the children an example by starting with the child nearest to you and saying, 'What is your name?' The child might respond, 'John'. Ask 'John' to say his name again but this time to answer by replying, 'My name is John' and to clap the rhythm for 'John' (one clap). Then, depending on the maturity of the class, either you or 'John' should turn to the next child and repeat the routine: 'What is your name?' 'My name is Poonam'. Poo-nam (two claps).'

Continue until all the children have had a turn.

Next, shift the focus to listening to the number of syllables in the names by asking the children to listen carefully, because some of them are going to be asked their names again and to clap their rhythm. Tell them that there is something special about all the rhythms that they are now going to hear. Use the question/answer routine to ask all the children with one-syllable names to clap their names. Then hold a short discussion to see if the children have spotted the connection between all these names. Lead the discussion by asking questions such as 'How many claps did John use?' and so on. Repeat the same routine with children with two-syllable names and so on.

To conclude, go round the group again, this time clapping the question instead of speaking it, and ask the children to clap the answer as well as their name (clap, clap, clap, clap – 'What is your name?' clap, clap, clap clap-clap – 'My name is Su-san.'). They can now communicate by rhythm!

Suggestion(s) for extension

During the main activity encourage the children to consider whether they think the number of claps has anything to do with the length of the name. See if the children can think of names of their friends or pets and clap their rhythms. The children could work in small groups to prepare variations on the activity to present to the whole group as a quiz. Working with the question/answer format these children might try: 'Who is your friend?' 'My friend is...' or 'What food do you like?' 'I like...' They could then record their presentation on a cassette.

Suggestion(s) for support

Some children will find it easier to clap the question and answers as well as their name. This gives them a 'run in'. It might help if the teacher carries out the question part of the routine around the whole group, freeing these children to focus on the answer. If necessary clap their name pattern with them, possibly holding their hands to give them confidence and to ensure that they make a simultaneous connection between the spoken word and the syllabic pattern. Ask the child to say their name slowly, exaggerating the parts that they can hear.

Assessment opportunities

This activity will reveal which children can and which cannot hear the syllables in their names. Through discussions they will identify that some names have the same number of syllables but that others are different. Some children may establish a link between the length of a word and the number of syllables in it.

SPELLING AND PHONICS KS1

Syllables

Opportunities for IT
Children could use a tape recorder to prepare and record some of their own clapping syllables. The work would require children to operate the tape recorder by recording their ideas, re-winding and listening and editing to present it to the class as a whole.

Display ideas
Make a cassette with the children which they can listen to.

Aspects of the English PoS covered
Speaking and listening – 1a; 2b.
Reading – 2b.

SORTING OUT NAMES

To recognise and distinguish monosyllabic words from polysyllabic words. To introduce the term 'syllable'.
†† *Whole class or small group.*
🕐 *30 minutes.*

Previous skills/knowledge needed
Children should have experience of rhythm through singing, dancing, clapping games, poetry and through playing percussion instruments. Children should realise that rhythmic patterns can be the same in some words and vary in others.

Key background information
Children's strong predisposition to rhythm can be used to help develop their awareness of syllables. Marie Clay (1993) has shown that children can become more aware of syllables by clapping or tapping out the sounds they can hear. Saying words slowly and emphasising the segments that they can hear can also help children to distinguish syllables. Only after they have had plenty of experience of working with syllables orally will children begin to make sense of them in the written form. Children need plenty of experience of working with words and talking about them to develop their understanding that some words consist of more syllables than others. In these discussions, continually using the word 'claps' rather than 'syllable' may prove rather clumsy and unclear. This activity provides a natural way in which children can be introduced to using the term 'syllable'. Of course, to provide them with awareness of the term 'syllable' is one thing but it will take time for the concept to develop fully.

Preparation
Draw up a bar chart for the extension activity.

Resources needed
Flip chart, blank name cards, photocopiable page 140, sheet of A1-size paper, writing and art materials.

What to do
Start the session by working with the children's names. Go quickly around the group and ask them to clap the rhythm of their names. Play a short preliminary sorting game where all the children with one-syllable names are asked to make 'one clap' to represent their names. Repeat the routine with all the children with two-syllable names, who should be asked to make 'two claps', and continue until all the children have heard their names categorised by the number of claps.

Now tell the children that in this activity they are going to sort their names into different groups according to the number of claps which they can hear in their names. Explain that there is a special word, 'syllables', which we can use to talk about the parts of words that we can hear. Give examples by using several names, first by clapping the syllables and then using the terminology, for example 'Jen-nif-er has three claps or we can say three syllables.' Then, using the flip chart, begin listing the children's names according to the number of syllables they contain. Start by asking the children with one-syllable names to identify themselves. Write a heading on the flip chart, 'These children have one syllable in their names,' and then compile the list. Once this has been completed move on to children with two-syllable names and so on. Use the clapping technique to accompany this part of the activity to support all the children.

Once the list is compiled ask the group to count up the number of children in each syllable group. Encourage the children to notice similarities between the words in each set and also to make comparisons between sets, eg. between words of one syllable and words of three syllables.

How many syllables are there in your name?

Syllables

A quick concluding activity will be to make cards for a 'Syllables Name Game'. This simply involves each child writing their name carefully on a blank name card, and illustrating it if they wish. On the back of the card the children should write a number to represent the number of syllables in their name. The game can be played as a variation on 'Happy Families'.

Suggestion(s) for extension

Some children could work with the data collected on the flip chart and convert this into a simple pictograph or bar chart. (The chart will need preparing in advance for them – see 'Preparation'.) They may like to compile this information on a computer using a data handling programme. They could then go on to make a set of question cards to accompany the chart, such as 'How many people have names of one syllable?' Alternatively, the children could complete photocopiable page 140 which asks them to collect fresh data about the number of syllables in people's names.

Suggestion(s) for support

Children requiring more practice with the main part of the activity can work with the teacher to compile simple wall charts for display. On a blank sheet of A1 paper write the heading, 'These children have one syllable in their names.' Ask the group whether they can remember which of the children had one-syllable names. As they offer names, list them under the heading. Then move on to the two-syllable names and so on. (The original list compiled on the flip chart can be used as a reference point for checking the lists either during or after this part of the activity.)

As the children work on the names, encourage them to 'stretch' out the polysyllabic words to help them hear the syllables. Ask them to say the words slowly and clearly, exaggerating the bits that they can hear. They can also tap or count the syllables as they analyse the words. As each list is completed, draw the children's attention to the features of the words, eg. length, and ask them to take turns to point to where the syllable 'breaks' come.

Assessment opportunities

Children can be assessed in terms of their ability to hear and clap syllables in names, whether they can successfully specify the number of syllables in names and whether they can begin to use the term 'syllable' as they talk about words. Children's growing confidence in categorising words by syllables should also be recorded. In addition, their comments on similarities and differences between the sets of names will also reveal their growing understanding of syllables. Errors and 'not sures' should also be noted in order to highlight possible areas of difficulty.

Opportunities for IT

Children could collect information about the different names in their class, or in other classes and use a simple database to record and display their information.

If a database is used it could have three fieldnames:

forename *Angela*
syllables *3*
sex *girl*

By adding the gender fieldname children can then look for patterns and differences between girls and boys names, for example:

whose name has the most syllables?
how many boys names have three syllables?
do more boys have three syllable names than girls?

Children might go on to look at names from different generations to see if they have changed. If a fourth field is added (year of birth) these names could be added to the existing database. The activity could lead to other kinds of questioning to look at how names have changed over the years.

The information found could be printed out in graphical format showing, for example, a block graph of the number of names with different numbers of syllables.

Display ideas

Give the graph a suitable title and display it on the wall. Place the quiz cards made in the extension activity on a small table near the graph so that the children can work in pairs to consolidate their knowledge. The wall charts made in the support activity will provide a reference list and can be added to as children think of other names, for example children in other classes or members of their own families.

Aspects of the English PoS covered

Speaking and listening – 1a.
Reading – 2b.
Writing – 2d; 3b.

Reference to photocopiable sheet

Photocopiable page 140 asks children to write down a list of names and to sort them according to the number of syllables they contain. Photocopiable page 141 is an assessment sheet.

THE SYLLABLES NAME GAME

To identify and talk about the distinguishing features of mono- and polysyllabic words in both their oral and written form.

†† *Small group.*

🕐 *20 minutes.*

Previous skills/knowledge needed

Children should know that words have rhythmic patterns or syllables and that some words have more syllables than others.

Key background information

Initially, children identify syllables in words by listening and saying words aloud. Marie Clay (1993) suggests that 'stretching' words out to exaggerate the segments can help them hear the different parts of words more clearly. This takes a lot of practice. Connecting the segments that they hear in words with the graphic form can prove challenging and confusing. It is important, therefore, for children to have the opportunity to discuss these confusions and resolve them with the teacher's help. A significant breakthrough for children is the discovery that some words have the same number of syllables but other words can be differentiated from them by having a different number of syllables. They will also discover that although the length of a word can indicate the number of syllables it contains this is not always the case. Children need to look closely at how the letter patterns fall within syllables, in particular the placing of vowels. Sorting words into sets will help them make many of these important comparisons.

This activity is targeted at children who have difficulty identifying the number of syllables in familiar names and words. The aim is to provide them with opportunities for additional practice at identifying mono- and polysyllabic words.

Preparation

Ask each child in the class to make a name card or prepare a set in advance of the session. Write the number of syllables in the name on the back of each card. Cut some blank names cards for the extension activity. Prepare a set of number cards: '1', '2', '3', '4' and '?' to represent numbers of syllables. (The '?' card will be used for categorising 'don't knows/unsures'.) Make and display wall charts with all the children's names sorted into sets according to the number of syllables.

Resources needed

A set of name cards, a set of number cards, set hoops (optional), wall charts of children's names, blank cards, writing materials.

Syllables

What to do

Lay out the number cards '1', '2', '3', '4' and '?' on a table. The set hoops can also be used if you wish. Deal the name cards (name side up) to the group, including a set for the teacher. Tell the children that the numbers represent the number of syllables in the names and explain that the purpose of the game is to take turns to place each name card into the correct 'syllable group'. All the names should find a home. If, when their turn comes, they are unsure about any of the names they can place them in the '?' set and return to them later on.

Start the game by reading out the name on the first card, for example 'Jonathan'. Do this slowly and then ask, 'How many claps are there in Jonathan?' Help the children by saying the word in a manner which emphasises the syllables. Then, place 'Jonathan' in the three syllable set. Then it is the turn of the child on your right to read out one of her cards. The game continues until all the names have found a home. Any words place in the '?' set should be discussed and sorted at the end of the game. As the game progresses, encourage the children to discuss whether words have lots of syllables or a few. At the end of the activity they should notice which names have the same number of syllables.

To conclude the game turn all the cards over, set by set, to check that the number on the back of the cards tallies with the set that they have been placed in. Any errors should be carefully discussed with the children, who should be encouraged to check again for themselves. The wall charts will provide a point of reference for further double checking.

Suggestion(s) for extension

Working with the two-syllable set of cards, take the names in turn and ask the children to identify where they think the first syllable ends and the second syllable starts. Do this first by saying the word aloud and then look at the printed form. Talk about the features of the two-syllable names, encouraging the children to comment on what they notice. A child may comment that most names seem to split either side of the middle of a word, as in 'Nir-mal' or 'Les-ley', but that there are also exceptions, such as 'Y-vonne'. The children could also notice whether consonants or vowels tend to start the second syllable and they should be encouraged to look carefully at the incidence of vowels within syllables. They might also find it interesting to count the length of the two-syllable names (usually six or seven letters, but what about 'Adam' or 'Amy'?).

Suggestions(s) for support

Ask each child to suggest other names, such as those of brothers, sisters, parents and pets. If they know how to spell the names, ask them to write them on individual cards. If they need help then write the words out for them. Once the new name cards have been made ask the children to say the names aloud and decide on the number of syllables. Then they can place the cards in the appropriate set or compile a fresh game for others to try.

Assessment opportunities

Children can be assessed by their ability to hear and clap and say syllables in names and the degree of confidence and accuracy with which they are able to sort the names into 'syllable sets'. Through a mini-quiz, for example, by asking questions such as 'How many syllables are there in John?', the children will reveal whether they can identify syllables in words automatically, without going through the clapping/ saying routines. In the extension activity children will

demonstrate their knowledge of whether they think syllable breaks come and notice common features about the letter patterns in syllables. They will also be identifying exceptions to these patterns. Notice whether children 'chunk' segments of words using the onset and rime as in 'Gr-ace' (the onset being 'Gr' and the rime 'ace').

Display ideas
The 'Syllables Name Game' cards and hoops can be displayed in the classroom and made available for additional practice. Notices inviting children to play the 'Syllable Name Game' should be displayed alongside.

Aspects of the English PoS covered
Speaking and listening – 1a; 2b.
Reading – 2a, b.

SEASIDE SUITCASE

To provide children with experience of working with and listening to polysyllabic words. To help children understand that some two-syllable words are composed of two monosyllabic words.

✝✝ *Whole class or small group.*

🕐 *40 minutes.*

Previous skills/knowledge needed
Children will have to have had previous experience of a range of rhythmic activities, for example in music, clapping games and so on. They should have participated in activities where they have clapped familiar rhythms, such as their names, and will have noticed that some rhythmic patterns are similar and that others vary. Children should have worked with monosyllabic and two-syllable words in other activities and will have noticed that the break in two-syllable words can vary, as in 'A-my' and 'Des-mond'.

Key background information
The discovery that two or more words can combine together to create a new word is something that many children make when looking at the writing on the packaging of everyday items such as 'toothpaste' or 'teabag'. Through wordplay children will also combine words to create new compound words of their own. Many two-syllable compound words are constructed from two one-syllable words, which signals clearly to the child where the syllable breaks come, and this makes them a useful set of words to work with in introducing the idea of syllables.

Preparation
Select a range of items from each category on the 'Seaside Suitcase' resource sheet on photocopiable page 142 and place them in the suitcase. As far as possible use the genuine

articles or good quality photographs laminated on card. Label the suitcase 'Seaside Suitcase'.

Resources needed
A suitcase or rucksack, a selection of items from the 'Seaside Suitcase' resource sheet (photocopiable page 142), photocopiable page 143, flip chart, paper, writing and art materials.

What to do
Show the children the unopened suitcase and explain that it is called the 'Seaside Suitcase'. Inside are lots of items which need to be unpacked one by one. They will be helping with this but the items must be removed in a particular order as there is a story to tell as each set of items comes out. (The function of the story is simply to provide a meaningful context for thinking about the words.) The basics of the story are provided on the resource sheet, but you should elaborate and expand it as you wish. As each item is mentioned it should be removed from the suitcase and displayed.

Once the suitcase is empty ask the children to think carefully about the names of the items they have unpacked. Perhaps they have already noticed something about the words. Take some of the items and say their names slowly, for example 'handbag'. Ask the children if they notice anything. If not, try some more items, eg. 'toothbrush'. If the children do not identify the key feature that the names of these items are made up of two separate words, use one of the items to demonstrate. For example, with 'handbag' ask the children if they can hear one word or two. If they can hear two, what two words can they hear? Quickly sketch the 'hand' and the 'bag' on the flip chart. Then ask the children

Syllables

to work in pairs with one child saying the first half of the words and the other saying the second half. For example, with 'toothbrush' one child says 'tooth' and the other says 'brush'. Ask each pair to present their pair of words back to the whole group and then say the word as a whole again. Having ensured that all the children have had practice at identifying that two words combine to form a compound word, they are now ready to focus on the syllables.

Using one of the items, such as 'handbag', as an example ask the children to clap the rhythm of the word. How many claps did they need to do? Repeat this several times with the other words and then ask the children what they notice. If necessary, recapitulate along the following lines: '"Handbag" has two claps; "toothbrush" has two claps; "seaweed" has... how many claps? Yes, two as well. Why do you think all these words have two claps?' At this stage the children should return to the first key point of the session which was that all the words are composed of two words that have been joined together. If appropriate, encourage them to use the word 'syllable' to help them talk about the words. To conclude, the children can select an item each from the 'Seaside Suitcase' and draw pictures to represent the two words that form the single compound word, for example a 'tooth' and a 'brush'. These can then be labelled for display purposes.

Suggestion(s) for extension

Photocopiable page 143 contains a further set of compound words. The children should work in pairs to decide where the words split and illustrate each half. Alternatively, they could try 'The Clapping Game' (see page xxx) where they will discover that some names have the same number of syllables and that others have different syllabic patterns. Discuss why it is that all the compound words that they have just worked with had two syllables.

Suggestion(s) for support

Some children will benefit from warm-up activities working with syllables in familiar ways before proceeding to this activity. They will be helped by first carrying out some clapping rhymes and games and clapping the rhythm of their own and their friends' names. If, when they move on to the main activity, they still cannot identify the two words that form the compound word, ask them to say the words slowly and clap the rhythm at the same time. Demonstrate for them, pausing after the first syllable before moving on to the second. Ask the children to try the same technique.

Assessment opportunities

Through their responses to the questions posed above, the children will reveal whether they can/cannot distinguish the two words that combine to form the compound words. They will also show whether they can recognise the two syllables in the words and the consistency of the syllabic pattern. Some will be able to make comparisons with other syllabic patterns identified in other activities.

Display ideas

The suitcase and its contents can be displayed for the children to play with. The children's illustrations can form a wall display which would need to be labelled to indicate how the two words combine to form one word.

Aspects of the English PoS covered

Reading – 2b.

Reference to photocopiable sheets

The 'Seaside Suitcase' resource sheet on photocopiable page 142 contains the bare bones of a story and a list of items that may be found in the suitcase. Further compound words can be found on photocopiable page 143.

SPELLING AND
PHONICS KS1

Syllables

SEASIDE SUITCASE: SPELLING

That two single monosyllabic words can combine to form a new word of two syllables.

†† *Small group.*

🕐 *30 minutes.*

Previous skills/knowledge needed
Children will need a bank of monosyllabic words that they can recognise and spell. They may have noticed that some words can combine together to make new words.

Key background information
The discovery that two or more words can combine together to create a new word is something that many children make when looking at the writing on the packaging of everyday items, such as a tube of toothpaste. They may even complain that whoever wrote the words forgot to leave a gap. Through wordplay children will also combine words to create new compound words of their own. Many two-syllable compound words are constructed from two one-syllable words, which signals clearly to the child where the syllable breaks come and thus makes them attractive and simple to work with.

Preparation
Select a range of items from each category on the 'Seaside Suitcase' resource sheet on photocopiable page 142 and place in the suitcase. If some of the genuine articles are unobtainable then substitute with good quality photographs laminated on card. Stick a large label on the suitcase saying 'Seaside Suitcase'. Write a list of all the items to be used on the flip chart; write the names of each of the items on cards (two cards for each item, for example, 'tooth' and 'brush') and attach velcro or magnetic tape to the back. Photocopy enough 'Can You Pack the Seaside Suitcase?' sheets (photocopiable pages 144 and 145) for the extension activity.

Resources needed
A suitcase, a selection of items from the 'Seaside Suitcase' resource sheet, a set of name cards of the items, tie-on luggage labels containing the names of the items used, magnet board or flannelgraph, flip chart, scissors, adhesive.

What to do
Show the pupils the unopened suitcase and explain that it is called the 'Seaside Suitcase'. Inside are lots of items to be unpacked from the suitcase one by one. The children's help will be needed to remove the items from the suitcase, but this has to be done in a particular order as there is a story to tell as each set of items is taken out. (The function of the story is simply to provide a meaningful context for looking at words.) The basics of the story are provided on the 'Seaside Suitcase' resource sheet on photocopiable page xxx, but you should elaborate and expand it as you wish. As each item is mentioned in the story ask the children to take turns to remove it from the case.

Once the items have been unpacked ask the children to say some of the words again slowly, listening carefully as they do so. Starting, for example, with 'hand-bag', ask them how many syllables they can hear in 'handbag'. Then ask them to clap the rhythm. Move on to the next word, for example 'milkshake', and repeat the routine. What do they notice about the words? As well as noticing that all the words have two syllables, the children should realise that each word is a combination of two separate words. Go round the group asking the children to take turns to say one of the compound words clearly. They should then try to identify the two words that they can hear which combine to form the compound word. Using the set of word cards look at the items again and display the words on the magnet board or flannelgraph. Ask the children to take turns to point out the two words within each compound word as they are displayed.

For the final part of the activity remove all the cards and shuffle them in preparation for playing a short domino-style card game called 'Word Hunt'. Explain to the children that all the words have now been mixed up and that they are going to take turns to help find the complete words again. Deal all the cards out and ask the children to take a few minutes to look at their cards. If they can remake some of the words they should do so and place them face up as a complete word on the table. Once this sorting stage has been completed, the first child should look at his incomplete words and ask the person next to him for one of his missing words, for example: 'I've got "tooth", have you got "paste"?' If he is successful the first child then takes another turn. If not, the turn moves to the next player. Continue the game until all the words have been reunited. •

Syllables

Suggestion(s) for extension

Several of the compounds have the same first syllable word, for example 'tooth', 'head', 'sea' and 'tea'. Ask the children to rearrange the order of the 'Seaside Suitcase' words so that those with the same first syllable are grouped together. Can they add some more words to these groups, such as 'seaside', 'teatime', or 'headache'? Which part of these words changes when a new word is made, and which part stays the same? What do they notice about the length of the compound words? The children may comment that some of the words have the same number of letters, such as 'tea' and 'pot' or 'rain' and 'coat', but some, like 'sea' and 'horse', are different lengths. Can they sort the words out again according to length?

Finally, put the children in pairs, provide scissors and glue and give each pair a copy of the 'Can You Pack The Seaside Suitcase?' sheets on photocopiable pages 144 and 145. Explain to the children that each of the luggage labels on the first sheet only contains the first half of the word. Read these words through with the children. Tell them that the second half of the words are on the second sheet. The children will have to cut these out and stick them on the correct luggage label on the first sheet to complete each word.

Suggestion(s) for support

Some children will need to work with a limited quantity of items and words. (Allow enough items to go evenly around the children when they are paired up later on.) This time the items can come out of the suitcase with their names written on luggage labels. Place the items in the middle of the table. Repeat the main activity as before, saying the compound words aloud, listening for and identifying the words and looking at and discussing the words as they go on the magnet board or flannelgraph. Then pair the children up and shuffle the word cards as before, but place them in a pile in the middle of the table. Ask each pair in turn to take a seaside

item from the middle of the table until all the items have been removed. The children's 'Word Hunt' will then focus on their specific items. Ask the first pair to take a card from the top of the pile and read it, for example 'tooth'. The children should look at the items and decide who has got something that starts with the word 'tooth'. The card should then be placed by the correct item. If the first pair has the item they take another card; if not, the next pair has their turn. The game concludes when all the compound words have been made and matched to their items.

Assessment opportunities

Through participating in the activities the children will demonstrate the extent of their understanding that compound words are made up of two other words. They will show their flexibility at combining words and, through their errors and subsequent explanations, justify why some choices are unsuitable. Some children will comment on the length of the pairs of words and will recognise that more than one compound word can use the same root word to make a new word. Children experiencing difficulty will use strategies such as 'matching' words to help them succeed in the activities. Some children will notice that all the words in the suitcase contain the same number of syllables.

Opportunities for IT

This activity could be extended by using framework software such as My World. The teacher could set up the suitcase words using the software and children could then move the various parts on to the working area of the screen to match them to create the compound words. The ease of dragging the different words will enable children to edit and rearrange the words they have created, and to print out their final version at the end of the session. Different scenarios could be set up in different files using, for example, a kitchen or bedroom theme.

82

SPELLING AND PHONICS KS1

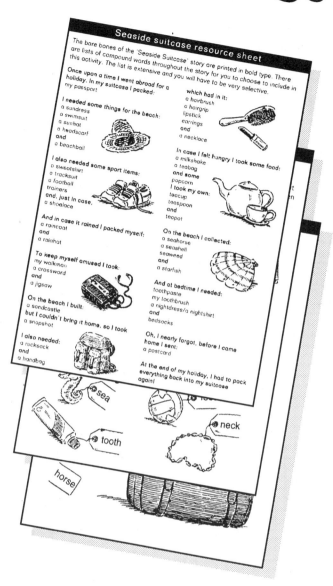

Seaside suitcase resource sheet

The bare bones of the 'Seaside Suitcase' story are printed in bold type. There are lists of compound words throughout the story for you to choose to include in this activity. The list is extensive and you will have to be very selective.

Once upon a time I went abroad for a holiday. In my suitcase I packed:
my passport

I needed some things for the beach:
a sundress
a swimsuit
a sunhat
a headscarf
and
a beachball

I also needed some sport items:
a sweatshirt
a tracksuit
a football
trainers
and, just in case,
a shoelace

And in case it rained I packed myself:
a raincoat
and
a rainhat

To keep myself amused I took:
my walkman
a crossword
and
a jigsaw

On the beach I built:
a sandcastle
but I couldn't bring it home, so I took
a snapshot

I also needed:
a rucksack
and
a handbag

which had in it:
a hairbrush
a hairgrip
lipstick
earrings
and
a necklace

In case I felt hungry I took some food:
a milkshake
a teabag
and some
popcorn
I took my own:
teacup
teaspoon
and
teapot

On the beach I collected:
a seahorse
a seashell
seaweed
and
a starfish

And at bedtime I needed:
toothpaste
my toothbrush
a nightdress/a nightshirt
and
bedsocks

Oh, I nearly forgot, before I came home I sent:
a postcard

At the end of my holiday, I had to pack everything back into my suitcase again!

sea
tooth
neck
horse

POLYSYLLABIC CREATURES

To provide children with experience of analysing the sounds in polysyllabic words with a particular focus on words of three syllables.

♦♦ *Small group.*
🕐 *20–30 minutes.*

Previous skills/knowledge needed
Children will need experience of a range of activities involving rhythm, including songs, clapping, and dancing games. They will need experience of listening for syllables in words and should have sorted a known set of words by the number of syllables that they can hear. Familiarity with the terms 'consonant' and 'vowel' will be necessary for discussion.

Key background information
This activity will introduce the term 'syllable' to talk about the parts of words. Although children may have been able to identify syllables orally, the division of written words into syllables is rather more problematic. Linguists disagree about the precise definition of a syllable, but at this stage the definition which stages that 'a syllable must contain a vowel (including 'y') with or without an opening or terminal consonantal group' will be useful.

Display ideas
The suitcase, items and labels can be set up as an interactive display. The quantity of items can steadily be increased as the children gain confidence. As the children retell the 'Seaside Suitcase' story they can match the luggage labels to the correct items. The magnet board or flannelgraph and accompanying cards can also be left available for further practice.

Aspects of the English PoS covered
Reading – 2b.
Writing – 2d.

Reference to photocopiable sheets
The 'Seaside Suitcase' resource sheet is on page 142. This lists items that may be found in the suitcase and the bare bones of a story. Other interesting groups of compound words are also listed to support similar activities. The 'Can You Pack the Seaside Suitcase?' sheets on photocopiable pages 144 and 145 contain single syllable words which combine to make compound words on luggage labels.

Syllables

Preparation

Copy photocopiable page 146 on to card or paste a copy on to card. Laminate it and cut out the individual cards as indicated. Write on the flip chart the names that you are going to use in the main activity.

Resources needed

Creature cards (see 'Preparation'), flip chart, pens, dry white markers, ruler, scissors, highlighter pens. If the 'Syllables Name Game' has been played, the cards from this game could be referred to.

What to do

The aim of this activity is to help children focus on what they can hear when they separate longer words into syllables. Start the activity by reminding them of previous occasions in which they have clapped the number of syllables in names, (for example, they may have played the 'Syllables Name Game', page 77). As a warm-up, hold a brief quiz, asking questions such as 'How many syllables can you hear in Jonathan?', 'Can you clap them?', 'Can you say the different parts of his name?' and so on. Then explain that in this session the focus is going to be on the names of some creatures which just happen to contain the same number of syllables.

Read out a selection of the creatures from photocopiable page 146. Start with the name of the first creature and ask the first child in the group to clap the rhythmic pattern of the word. Ask the child how many claps she made and tell her to remember the name of her creature. Go on to the next child and repeat the procedure until everyone has clapped the

rhythm of their own creature. Compare notes on the number of syllables in the words, which the children should agree to be three.

Next, demonstrate the second part of the activity which involves articulating the sounds that the children can hear in each syllable, for example 'por-cu-pine'. Point to the word 'porcupine' on the flip chart and indicate how the sounds relate to the segments of the word. Use a different-coloured pen to mark the different segments, 'por/cu/pine'. Check that the first child has remembered her creature and ask her to say the word slowly, emphasising each syllable. Using the pen, mark and read out the different syllables of the word. Once all the children have had a go at sounding their word, look at the chart and discuss the different segments of the words. Encourage the children to discuss the bits they may not have been sure about, for example the middle segment of the words. Depending on the experience of the group, it may be appropriate to discuss the role of vowels in polysyllabic words, particularly in the middle syllables. (This is developed in the 'Suggestions(s) for extension'.)

Finally, give the children their prepared 'Polysyllabic Creatures Card'. Explain that they should cut up their word into its three syllables. Using a ruler and a dry white marker show how they should rule two lines to separate the syllables.

Syllables

this activity could go on to work with words of four or more syllables.

Suggestion(s) for support
Some children will find it difficult to make the connection between what they can hear and the graphic representation of the syllables. Ask these children to say their creature's name slowly, emphasising the three segments. As they say each syllable write it down for them so that they can see the word forming before their eyes. It might also help to ask these children to identify the syllable that they can distinguish most clearly and then return to the parts of the words that they find more difficult. Repeat the activity with other words on the list and, if necessary, work with some two-syllable words, such as 'monkey' or 'rabbit', to make the task easier.

Assessment opportunities
The children can be assessed on their confidence in identifying the number of syllables in their word. Some children may continue to find this difficult. The way in which they split the word orally into segments will reveal the sounds that they can hear in the word. Their response as they see the word 'boxed' on the chart, or as they see the word written as they identify the syllables, will also provide information. Other ways of segmenting or chunking the words should also be noted, for example if they try to sound letter to letter (synthetically).

The children's comments on the parts of the words that they are unsure of should be recorded as should their insights on vowels.

Suggestion(s) for extension
In the main activity, when all the creatures' names have been scribed on to the flip chart and marked to show their different segments, encourage the children to look carefully at the way the vowels are positioned in the different syllables. Using a highlighter pen ask the children to help spot the vowels. Help them to see how the vowels tend to appear in each syllable and draw their attention particularly to the role of the vowels in the middle syllable. The children could say which vowels they can hear clearly, such as the 'i' in 'pelican' or the 'o' in 'dinosaur', and then compare these with the 'ter' in 'butterfly'. They may notice that in this set of words vowels are usually followed by a consonant, the exception being 'au' in the 'saur' part of 'dinosaur'. The spelling of the syllable 'saur' may provoke lively debate. Discuss any logical alternative spellings, such as 'saw', that the children may offer. Children showing confidence in

Creature cards

antelope	dinosaur	nightingale
buffalo	elephant	octopus
butterfly	gorilla	parakeet
centipede	kangaroo	pelican
crocodile	Labrador	porcupine
chimpanzee	mosquito	unicorn

Display ideas
A display, with the title 'Polysyllabic Creatures', can be created using large photographs of as many of the creatures as possible, along with cards bearing their names with the syllable breaks marked, and an invitation to 'count the syllables'.

Aspects of the English PoS covered
Reading – 2b.

Reference to photocopiable sheet
Photocopiable page 146 contains a set of cards with three-syllable creatures' names. It is suggested that teachers work with a limited selection of these.

Syllables

CREATURES CARD GAME

To provide children with experience of analysing polysyllabic words. To provide them with opportunities to link the sounds they hear in syllables with their graphic form.

†† *Pairs or small group.*

🕐 *15 minutes.*

Previous skills/knowledge needed

Children will need experience of listening to rhythm in words in a variety of contexts, for example rhymes, songs and music, and should have considered differences in rhythmic patterns in words of different syllabic length. They will have to have had some experience of the term 'syllable'. It will be helpful if they have met and used the term 'vowel'. Experience of relating the sounds that they can hear in syllables to their written form will be helpful as will experience of looking at words analytically in terms of their syllabic structure.

Key background information

Although children may have been able to identify syllables orally, the division of written words into syllables is rather more problematic. Linguists disagree about the precise definition of a syllable, but at this stage the definition which stages that 'a syllable must contain a vowel (including 'y') with or without an opening or terminal consonantal group' will be useful.

Preparation

Copy photocopiable page 146 on to card or paste a copy on to card. Laminate the page and cut out the individual cards. Then cut the cards into their individual syllables. Make another set of cards in the same way but leave the words whole.

Resources needed

A set of creature name cards cut into syllables and a duplicate set of the complete words (see 'Preparation'), flip chart and pens.

What to do

Remind the group of the work they have done on syllables. Remind them how words are divided into syllables and demonstrate with one of the cards, if necessary. Show them the cards that have been made and explain that they are to rebuild the words that have been separated into syllables. Before commencing the game, run through the complete list of words that they are trying to make and write the list on the flip chart as a point of reference. Explain that first time through the game they will work together to rebuild the words. Provide the children with an example of what is required by showing them how some of the cards fit together to remake complete words. In doing this it is important to talk about the beginning, middle and end of the words and to use the term 'syllable'. Encourage the children to help in this initial part of the activity and to ask questions.

Shuffle all the cards and stand the deck in the middle of the table. Ask the first child to pick up the card on the top of the pile and lay it face up on the table. Ask the child whether she thinks the syllable she has picked up is a beginning, middle or end (the structure of the letters should provide a clear indication). If the child is unsure, ask the others in the group to help. Can anyone read the sound on the card? Which word might it be part of? Draw attention to the word on the flip chart or use the complete word card from the duplicate set to check hypotheses. Having established whether it is a beginning, middle or end of the word, the second child in the group should pick up the next card on the deck. The children must then decide together whether the syllable belongs to the first word or is part of another word. If it belongs to the same word as a previous card it must be given to the holder of that word. If not, the card is retained to become the word that this player is collecting. The game continues until all the syllables have been put together to form complete words.

To conclude, reshuffle the cards, deal them out and play the game on an individual, rather than group basis.

Suggestion(s) for extension

Once all the cards have been played ask the children to look carefully at the syllables and encourage them to comment on the frequency of vowels in each of the syllables. They should also be asked to comment on the length of most of the words. Ask the children to select three of the words which they think they can spell. When they are ready they should turn the words over and try spelling them from memory. Ask them first to try to spell the words aloud and then to use a pencil and paper to help them. If they are struggling remind them to think about the three syllables in each of the words and to remember that each syllable will

86

SPELLING AND PHONICS KS1

Syllables

gor / e / lope

un / i / roo

have at least one vowel in it. Having tried the words, they should check them against the word cards. Finally, the children could play the whole card game as a 'solo' activity.

Suggestion(s) for support

Some children may find the word game difficult and should therefore work with just a few words and be encouraged to use the duplicate set of word cards to support them as they try to reconstruct the words. Draw their attention to the combination of letters in the syllable and encourage them to consider whether the syllable is likely to come at the beginning, middle or end of the word. These children may find the 'Seaside Suitcase: spelling' activity (page xxx) a more supportive alternative, as it works with clearly defined two-syllable words. Some children will benefit more by doing some of the activities which emphasise listening to words, and clapping the segments that they can hear.

Assessment opportunities

The main method of assessment will be through observing the children playing the card game and listening to their comments and questions as they play. It will be of specific interest to note how effectively they identify beginning, middle and final syllables and what strategies they employ to do this, for example sounding the syllable out loud, checking it against the flip chart or duplicate cards, or by commenting on the graphic patterns in the syllable. Some children will be able to use their knowledge of syllables to spell three-syllable words. They may also attempt to use vowels in each segment of the word. Their errors and hypotheses about spelling the words should be carefully monitored.

Display ideas

The cards can be displayed for further independent games, together with pictures of the creatures.

Aspects of the English PoS covered

Reading – 2b.

Reference to photocopiable sheet

Photocopiable page 146 provides a set of creatures' names with three syllables.

Creature cards

antelope	dinosaur	nightingale
buffalo	elephant	octopus
butterfly	gorilla	parakeet
centipede	kangaroo	pelican
crocodile	Labrador	porcupine
chimpanzee	mosquito	unicorn

87

SPELLING AND PHONICS KS1

Syllables

YOU GO HOME!

To consolidate children's knowledge of syllables and to help them make this knowledge explicit.

†† *Small groups.*

🕐 *20 minutes.*

Previous skills/knowledge needed

Children will have to have participated in a range of activities that explore rhythm in words. They should have listened for syllables, said the sounds that they can hear in syllables and worked with syllables in their graphic form. Children need to have worked with both mono- and polysyllabic words. They need some experience of looking at words analytically and physically taking words apart and putting them back together again.

Key background information

This activity, along with others, aims to develop familiarity with the terminology needed to talk about words and their spellings. The terms 'syllable', 'vowel', 'consonant' will be needed in all activities to do with syllables.

Preparation

Make four sets of cards of familiar words (12 words in each set). Each set should represent a specific syllabic group, that is set 1 should contain one-syllable words, set 2 should contain two-syllable words, and so on. Make four 'homes' for the sets of the syllables (these should be attractively covered open containers). The 'homes' should have a number on the front to represent the number of syllables in the words that they will be storing. Make dice with numbers up to four (numbers on the dice may need to be adjusted according to the number of syllables being worked with). Before commencing the game decide how many sets of cards the children are able to work with, for example beginners may cope best with using just two sets of words at a time.

Resources needed

Sets of cards with 'homes' (see 'Preparation'), spare card, pens, dictionaries.

What to do

Before starting this activity it may be necessary briefly to review with the group some of the key points about syllables. This might include listening for words of different syllabic length and familiarising the group with the sets of words which are to be used in this activity.

The purpose of the game is for *everyone* to collect words which have the *same* number of syllables. The number of syllables for each game is determined at the start by rolling the dice. Take the sets of syllable cards and shuffle them. Place them in the middle of the table. Show the children the empty 'homes' and point out the numbers on them – there will not be a 'home' for the set(s) which will be collected. Having rolled the dice, explain that in this round of the game they are only going to collect words of, say, three syllables. If they turn up a card that does not have three syllables they must say, 'You Go Home!' and put the card as quickly as possible into the correct 'home' box. If, as the game is played,

they think that another player has made an error, they can halt the round by saying 'Challenge' and explaining what they think the error is. If the 'challenge' is correct, the challenger takes an extra card on their next turn. The winner of the game is the person who, at the end, has collected the most cards (in this example, of three-syllable words). At the very end of the game ask the children in pairs to check each of the 'home' boxes for errors and to make corrections. The game can then be played again.

Suggestion(s) for extension

Having completed a round of the game, play a quick quiz with the group. Start with a confident member of the group and ask them to roll the dice. When they see the number on the dice they must think of a word with the appropriate number of syllables. Move on round the group. If children lack confidence they can work in pairs. A further variation would be for the child, having thought of a word, to then say the word aloud, emphasising the syllables, and try to write it down. The rest of the group could also try to write the word and then compare their results. Finally, see if the group can think of some really long words (four syllables or more) which could be used to make another set of syllable cards. Write down their suggestions for them.

Suggestion(s) for support

The main activity can readily be adapted for paired 'teams'. Children who are inexperienced or lack confidence should work with familiar words that follow regular phonic patterns. The teacher will need to judge how many sets of words to use at once. Children in difficulties should be encouraged to use familiar strategies, such as clapping the rhythm of the words and saying the words before they make a decision. The game could be played as a straightforward sorting activity. If they have difficulty working with a particular syllabic length, then use that set of word cards to provide further practice of talking about the words, saying them, listening to their rhythm and chopping them up into syllables.

Assessment opportunities

Some children will be operating at an 'automatic' level, that is they do not visibly use oral or physical strategies to help them make decisions. Others will be using a range of techniques to help themselves make choices about the

words. When children make 'challenges' note their argument for making changes. At the end of the session observe how errors are rectified. If children try the writing activity make a record of their attempts at spelling and, if errors occur, look closely to see whether these are logical, for example: a 'z' for an 's'. This will indicate areas of further support.

Display ideas

The 'You Go Home!' game could be put on an interest table for children to use for extra practice. A 'quiz' box could be made and blank postcards provided for the children to write questions to go with the game, for example: 'Think of a word of two syllables which starts with a 'd' and ends with a 'y'? (Donkey.) The answers should be written upside-down on the back of the card.

Aspects of the English PoS covered

Reading – 2b.

HAIKU

To apply children's knowledge of syllables to produce a specific form of written language.

†† *Small groups or whole class.*

⏲ *30–40 minutes.*

Previous skills/knowledge needed

Children should have experience of listening for rhythm in nursery rhymes or poetry and in familiar words such as their names. They will have to have looked at the rhythmic similarities and difference between words, for example through clapping and counting syllables. In their discussions they should have been introduced to the term 'syllable'.

Key background information

Writing haiku poetry is heavily dependent on using and applying knowledge of syllables. Haiku poetry originated in Japan in the sixteenth century and has a strict stylistic form which must be compiled with in order to achieve the appropriate poetic effect. Strictly, the poem should consist of seventeen syllables in total which are divided into three lines of poetry. The first line must be five syllables, the second

Syllables

seven and the third five again. The tight syllabic structure of this activity is intended to help children to think carefully about the word choices they make. As they construct their haiku they will need not only to select words to express their idea or image but also to consider the number of syllables in the words. As the poem is drafted, words may be rejected and replaced if they do not fit the syllabic pattern. The 'does it fit?' constraint will require the children to make explicit their knowledge and understanding of syllables.

Preparation

Make enough copies of photocopiable page 147 for each pair of children and of photocopiable page 148 for each child. If the theme for the individual poetry writing can be established ahead of the session then the children could be asked to bring in their own photographs or objects to support their work.

Resources needed

A world map, atlas or globe, information books on Japan (including some examples of Japanese script and traditional illustrations), colour photographs and/or objects based on the theme of pets, flip chart, writing materials, photocopiable pages 147 and 148, word processor, paper, art materials.

What to do

Using a selection of the resources listed above, set the context by showing the children where Japan is located on the map. Look briefly at some aspects of Japanese culture including the written language, which takes several years for their children to learn to write. Explain to the children that one of the things that the Japanese are very famous for is their talent for writing a particular kind of poetry called 'haiku'. Read out the following example, which is based on a pet cat:

> Sharp claws, bright green eyes (5)
> You catch birds in your strong jaws (7)
> Purring you sleep now. (5)

Then ask some questions about the poem: Did it sound like a poem? What was different? Did it take long to listen to? What did they think it was about? How did they know? What clues did the poem give them? It might also help to offer the children a clear contrast by reading them a verse of a rhyming poem or nursery rhyme and asking if they can notice some differences.

Working with the same haiku, write the poem up on the flip chart so that the children can see the layout. Indicate the line breaks by pausing. Involve the children in counting and numbering the lines and establish the rule that haiku poems always have three lines. Then go on to read each line in turn and ask the children to count the syllables. Check whether they counted correctly (each syllable could be numbered on the chart). It is important at this point to establish the five, seven, five rule. Ask the children to work in pairs to complete the 'Haiku poems' sheet on photocopiable page 147.

Syllables

Then, with the whole group, use the flip chart to compose a shared writing haiku, based on the theme of pets, using the photographs and/or objects as a stimulus. The aim of this part of the activity is to provide the group with a rehearsal for the next stage of the activity when they will try writing a haiku on their own. A good way of selecting possible words for the haiku is to look at the photograph and brainstorm possible words that it conjures up. These could then be used as a 'word bank' as the poem is composed. Encourage the children to think of words with similar meanings and write these up on the flip chart. In addition, it will be helpful to sort the words into sets of different numbers of syllables so that the children can quickly find a word that fits. When the shared writing is complete read the new haiku through with the children.

Tell the children that it is now their turn to write their own haiku on a topic of their choice. Once everyone has decided on their topic, give each child a copy of the 'My haiku poem' photocopiable sheet and explain that the sheet takes them through the same procedure that they have just used in the shared writing part of the activity. The children should first identify their topic: 'My haiku poem is about...' and then try to list as many words as they can think of which they might want to use in their poem. Once they have done this, they can pair up and share their ideas before composing their poem individually. As they complete their draft they should read it aloud to their partner and ask for feedback. Remind the children to check that their poem is three lines long and that each line contains the correct number of syllables.

To conclude, hold a poetry-reading session where all the children read out their poems to the rest of the class.

Suggestion(s) for extension

Ask the children to identify the word they used which had the highest number of syllables. If the children enjoyed writing haikus they could go on to try a variation of haiku called 'tanka' poems, which consist of five lines. The first three lines follow the normal haiku pattern with the sixth and seventh lines each being seven syllables long.

Suggestion(s) for support

Some children will benefit from working in pairs throughout the second part of the activity. This means that they will share the words that they brainstorm which can be scribed for them. In addition, it might help those children who are stuck for ideas to be provided with a first line to start them off. They may prefer to make up their haiku orally first before trying to put it down on paper.

Assessment opportunities

The activity can be assessed at several points in order to establish how effectively the children are able to utilise their knowledge of syllables. They may reveal in the introductory part of the activity that they can hear and count syllables. During the shared writing sequence note which children can suggest words with the appropriate number of syllables to fit in a specific line. Some children will be able to make corrections if they notice that a line is too long or short.

Opportunities for IT

Children could write their haiku poems using a word processor. The limitations imposed by writing haiku means that there is a limited amount of keyboarding required by the children. They should be given opportunities,

SPELLING AND PHONICS KS1

Syllables

possibly in pairs, to originate their work using the word processor rather than typing in handwritten work. As their poem develops they will need to be able to move the cursor around the screen to edit and alter specific words without deleting large portions of their text.

If children have access to a talking word processor they can use it to listen to their poem as it progresses and also to check the number of syllables they have used. If they set the speech facility to a slow speed it will give them more time to listen to the syllables.

Once the poems have been completed children could experiment with different font styles and sizes in order to make their poem more attractive for display in the classroom or for inclusion in a class book of haiku poems.

Display ideas

The completed haikus can be word processed and placed in a special book. The children could try producing Japanese-style watercolour illustrations to accompany their poetry. Alternatively the children's poems could be incorporated into a large display about Japan/Japanese culture, art, artefacts.

Aspects of the English PoS covered

Speaking and Listening – 2b.
Reading – 2b.
Writing – 1c.

Reference to photocopiable sheets

Children should complete photocopiable page 147 in pairs. this asks them to look at a partictular haiku and to consolidate their knowledge about it. Photocopiable page 148 asks children to compose their own haiku poem.

SPELLING AND
PHONICS KS1

Graphic knowledge

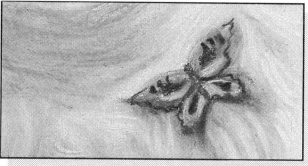

Although inexperienced writers will draw heavily on their alphabetic and phonic knowledge in attempting to spell, these strategies are often unreliable in English because there is not a consistent sound-letter correspondence. However, the spelling of words is not as illogical as may at first appear, and if children know something about constant letter-strings and word roots they are more likely to make an informed attempt at spelling. It is important therefore to focus attention on how words *look* rather than how they sound. Words with the same letter-strings should be grouped together, even though they sound different (for example *ea*, which may be said as in 'meat', 'pear', 'heart', 'bread'), rather than words which sound the same (for example 'meet', 'seat', 'piece', 'machine'), because these may contain a variety of letter strings.

The relationship between spelling and handwriting is also crucial. It is for this reason that, whatever handwriting style is used – and there is some evidence that joined-up writing may help in this respect – the actual writing of consistent letter-strings helps to fix them in the memory.

One of the most important factors in promoting both spelling development and word awareness is an interest in language. When they are very young, children naturally play with language and this delight in words – is a foundation on which teachers need to build. Language has many intriguing areas for investigation, from word origins to curious spellings, which children will enjoy exploring and in the process will learn much about how to spell.

SPELLING AND
PHONICS KS1

INTRODUCING CONSONANTS AND VOWELS

To introduce children to the terms 'consonant' and 'vowel'.

†† *Main activity: whole class or small group and then individual activity.*

🕐 *40 minutes: 25 minutes in whole group discussion; 15 minutes individual work.*

Previous skills/knowledge needed

Children will have to have had plenty of experience of the alphabet and its uses and should have some experience of using the alphabet to talk about words and their structure. They may have heard the terms 'consonant' and 'vowel' used by the teacher.

Key background information

Children need a metalanguage to enable them to talk about and reflect upon words. A metalanguage is language used to talk about language. Children need to be able to use the terms 'vowel' and 'consonant' when they discuss the structure of words, particularly in the context of spelling. By being able to analyse words in terms of vowels and consonants children will discover significant facts about the spelling system, for example that virtually all words contain vowels as well as consonants.

Preparation

Make a set of alphabet cards with the five vowels on different-coloured card. Make a set of name cards for all the children in the class and laminate them. Label one of the A1 sheets 'The Set of Consonants' and the second A1 sheet 'The Set of Vowels'. List the alphabet on the flip chart. Copy the worksheet on photocopiable page 149 for the extension activity.

Resources needed

Alphabet and name cards (see 'Preparation'), two sheets of A1 paper, flip chart, copies of photocopiable page 149, writing materials, simple ABC books.

What to do

Start the session off by singing/reciting the alphabet. Explain that in this session the children will be looking at the alphabet and finding out about it. Start by asking the children to estimate the number of letters in the alphabet. Jot their estimates down on the flip chart and then ask them to help check their estimates by counting the letters together. Count the letters which have been written on the flip chart and then write the number 26 on the flip chart. Establish with the children that they already know that the alphabet letters have names and that they also have sounds. At this point, encourage the children to demonstrate their knowledge. You could ask them questions such as: 'What is the name of the first letter of the alphabet? What is the sound made by the letter "f"? What is the name of the letter which makes a "p" sound? Do you know the name and the sound made by the 15th letter?'

Now explain that there is another way of talking about the alphabet and to do this we use two special words: 'consonants' and 'vowels'. Some children may have heard the terms before and will want to share their explanations. Establish that there are five vowels in the alphabet and that they are: 'a', 'e', 'i', 'o' and 'u'. Write them up on the flip chart and show the children where they fit into the alphabet. That leaves all the other letters which are known as 'consonants'. On 'The Set of Consonants' sheet prepared earlier ask the children to take turns to write down the

Suggestion(s) for extension

Continuing to work with their names, the children can complete the photocopiable worksheet on page 149. This requires them to count up the total number of letters in their names and then to work out how many of the letters are vowels and how many are consonants.

In further discussions encourage the children to look at how the vowels are positioned in their names, which letters combine and, in longer names, to look at the incidence of vowels within syllables. Encourage children to notice if other children have similar vowel or consonant patterns in their names.

Suggestion(s) for support

Help the children to set out the alphabet cards in sequence and then sort the letters into two sets: consonants and vowels. Encourage the children to identify the letters as they go along to check their alphabet knowledge. Count up the vowels and name them. Focus on the vowels and ask if they can think of a word that has an 'a' in it. Repeat the routine with the other vowels. Use the class name cards or simple ABC books to support this part of the activity.

Assessment opportunities

It is important in this activity to identify children who still have gaps in their knowledge of the alphabetic sequence and the names/sounds that the letters represent. Some children will make sense of distinguishing the consonants from the vowels and will apply this knowledge when they work with their name cards. These children may also be able to remember the names of the vowels. Others will reveal a limited understanding but may be able to identify vowels and consonants in their own names.

consonants. Use the ABC listed on the flip chart as a reference. Encourage the children to decide whether or not letters belong to 'The Set of Consonants'. Once completed, repeat the routine, using 'The Set of Vowels' sheet. Then remind the children that earlier on in the session they counted up the complete alphabet and that they found the total to be 26 letters. If there are five vowels in the alphabet, can anyone work out the number of consonants? Scribe the information on to the sheets and then display the two completed sheets in a prominent position as the children will now need to refer to them.

The final part of this activity is to help the children to use the terminology. Give out each child's name card and ask them to look at their name to see if they can find any vowels in it. How many can they find? What are the names of the vowels? Who has the most vowels in their name? Who has the least? Does anyone have no vowels in their name at all? Can the children think of any words that do not have vowels? Explore the reasons that the children give. Then discuss the consonants asking a similar range of questions.

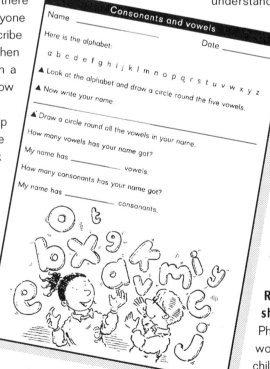

Name _____

Consonants and vowels

Here is the alphabet: Date _____

a b c d e f g h i j k l m n o p q r s t u v w x y z

▲ Look at the alphabet and draw a circle round the five vowels.

▲ Now write your name.

_____

▲ Draw a circle round all the vowels in your name.

_____

How many vowels has your name got?

My name has _____ vowels.

How many consonants has your name got?

My name has _____ consonants.

Display ideas

'The Set of Consonants' and 'The Set of Vowels' charts can form part of a display about the alphabet. The alphabet cards could be left out for further practice.

Aspects of the English PoS covered

Reading – 2a.
Writing – 2d.

Reference to photocopiable sheet

Photocopiable page 149 contains a worksheet that aims to develop children's knowledge of consonants and vowels.

The Set of Consonants

BCDFGH

NAME SORTING

*To provide experience of using the terms 'consonant'
and 'vowel' within a meaningful context. To
demonstrate the value of using metalanguage in order
to talk analytically about words and their structure.*

✝✝ *Small group or groups working in rotation.*

🕐 *30 minutes.*

Previous skills/knowledge needed

Childen will need knowledge of the alphabet and will have to
have used the letters and sounds of the alphabet to enable
them to talk about words and their structure. They should
have been introduced to the terms 'vowel' and 'consonant'
and have some experience of working with them.

Key background information

In order to analyse and discuss words, particularly in relation
to spelling, children need the appropriate terminology. The
terms 'consonant' and 'vowel' are essential for these
discussions. Although the need for appropriate terminology
is not required in the National Curriculum until Key Stage 2,
it is clearly beneficial for younger children to begin to develop
an awareness of terms that will be useful for them.

Preparation

Using two sheets of the A1 paper, make two charts for display
purposes with the headings 'The Set of Consonants' and
'The Set of Vowels'. On the consonant chart write the full
set of consonants and on the vowel chart write the vowels.
Using two more sheets of A1 paper prepare two further
charts, one with the heading 'These children's names start
with a vowel' and the other labelled 'These children's names
start with a consonant'. Make a set of name cards for all the

children in the class. The card used for the names should be
lightweight and cut to a suitable size so that the names can
be stuck on the two name charts. Make a set of alphabet
cards with the vowels on different-coloured card so that they
can be distinguished from the consonants.

Resources needed

Four sheets of A1 paper, name and alphabet cards (see
'Preparation'), writing materials, glue, set hoops.

What to do

Start by checking the children's familiarity with the alphabet.
Ask the children about vowels and consonants, gauging from
their responses how much they can remember. Then, use
the 'Set of Vowels' chart and the 'Set of Consonants' chart
and ask the children to write the letters of the alphabet on to
the appropriate chart. An alternative to using the charts would
be to sort the alphabet cards into two sets: vowels and
consonants. Next, give the children their own name cards
and spend some time searching for and discussing the vowels
and consonants.

Then introduce the key idea for this session which is to
practise looking for vowels and consonants by focusing on
the initial letter of the names of all the children in the class.
The full set of name cards will be needed for this part of the
activity. Using one of the children's names, demonstrate how
to look for initial vowels and consonants and refer to the
vowel and consonant charts to confirm whether the initial
letter is a vowel or a consonant. Introduce the two charts,
'These children's names start with a vowel' and 'These

children's names start with a consonant'. Show the children how to sort the names and how to decide whether the name cards should go on to the vowels chart or the consonant chart. Stick the first child's name card on to the appropriate chart. The second child should now take her turn, checking her name against the vowel and consonant charts. Continue until all the names have been sorted. The charts will now be ready to be displayed.

Suggestion(s) for extension
Once the name charts have been completed, ask the children to look at them and decide whether the majority of names start with a vowel or a consonant. Their findings could be followed up by surveying other classes in the school.

Then go on to look at the consonant chart and identify which consonant occurs most frequently as the initial sound of the children's names. Were all the consonants represented? If not, why not? This could lead to discussions about frequency of usage of some letters such as 'u', 'x' and 'z'. Carry out a similar discussion about the vowels.

Suggestion(s) for support
The children can work with set hoops and small quantities of name cards that are familiar to them in order to gain further experience of sorting the names by vowels and consonants. Lay out the alphabet cards on the table to help the children to check their decisions.

Assessment opportunities
As children carry out this activity you should observe and record:
▲ individual's knowledge of the alphabet;
▲ understanding of the distinction between vowel and consonant;
▲ ability to use appropriate terminology;
▲ ability to apply knowledge in identifying vowels and consonants in names.

Opportunites for IT
Children could create a simple database and use it to look at names that start with vowels or consonants and which are the most popular initial letters.

The database could be set up with just three fields:

name	*Balpinder*
vowel/consonant	*consonant*
sex	*boy*

The children could enter their own details into the database. They might also like to collect information from other classes in the school to extend the survey. To help them compare one class with another they could add a fourth fieldname, for example:

class	*2B*

Once the database has been set up children can search the database to find the most common initial letter:

How many names begin with the letter B?
Search on field 'name' begins with B and print the results
or
the names could be sorted into alphabetical order and the children could count the number beginning with B.

How many names begin with a consonant?
Search on field 'vowel/consonant' equals consonant and print the results.

This search could be displayed as a bar chart or pi graph to show the differences pictorially.

Display ideas
All the charts made in the session can be displayed and the alphabet cards made available for extra practice.

Aspects of the English PoS covered
Reading – 2a.

HAPPY FAMILY BLENDS

To focus on initial double consonant blends – 'st', 'sp', 'sw', 'sl', 'sm', 'sn', 'sc' and 'sk'. To encourage children to focus on visual pattern and 'sound' at the same time.

†† *Small group.*
🕐 *Up to 30 minutes.*

Previous skills/knowledge needed
Children need to have spent time working on initial letter activities. This activity is a development once single letters are known. It can be used for groups of children who may have made similar errors in writing these combinations. The children must be able to read all the words in the families, or they cannot ask for the cards. Since this game is fairly complicated to play, the players should have had some experience of playing similar games (for example, 'Happy Name Families', see page 28).

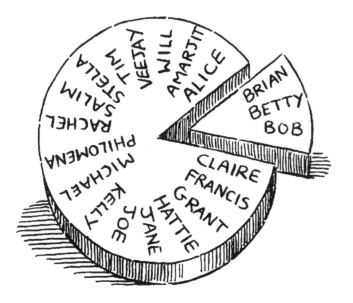

Key background information

This activity focuses on common initial blends with 's'. It is helpful to enable children to visualise letter patterns as well as to hear the sounds.

Preparation

Prepare a set of cards, each bearing a word beginning with one of the selected letter blends. You will need four words for each family; suggestions are offered in the table, but you may prefer to use specific words you would like the children to learn because they are commonly misspelled. A total of six to eight families will be needed. When you have decided which words and families you will use make a list of them and copy the list for each child.

's' followed by another consonant

st	sl	sw	sm	sn	sp	sc	sk
sting	slow	swing	small	snow	spell	scale	skate
stick	sleep	swim	smack	snip	spot	scar	skim
step	slug	swan	smile	snack	spin	scarf	skill
still	slip	sweep	smoke	snail	space	scare	skull
stay	slide	swallow	smash	snake	sparrow	scatter	sky
star	slug	swear	smell	snatch	spoil	school	skip
store	sledge	swift	smooth	snap	spend	scarlet	skid
stalk	slope	switch	smart	snore	speak	scamper	skirt
stone	slot	sweet	smudge	sniff	spare	scald	sketch

Resources needed

A set of families cards, a list of the words in each family for each player.

What to do

Ask one player to shuffle the cards and then deal them. The aim of the game is to collect all the cards in a particular family, for example – all the words beginning with 'st' or 'sk'.

Players sort their own hands into sets, putting together all the words they have beginning with each 'blend', and place these face down in front of them. They then look at each set in turn, checking with their families list to see which cards are needed in each set. They should try not to let the other players see the cards.

Starting to the left of the dealer, players take turns to ask other players for members of the family they aim to collect. Make sure they say 'please' and 'thank you' according to the normal rules of 'Happy Families', for example: 'Please, Peter, do you have "sting" from the "st" family?'

If Peter has the card, the recipient must say 'thank you' on receiving it and have another turn. If he does not have the card, he must say, 'Sorry, I haven't got "sting".' The turn then passes to him. If an asker forgets to say 'please' or 'thank you' he does not receive the card and the turn passes to the player he asked.

The winner is the player who collects the most complete family sets.

Suggestion(s) for extension

Challenge those children who find it easy to remember the words in the families to use a dictionary to find more of each family.

They could also be given a spelling challenge: in pairs, one partner could dictate the words and the other could see how many they can spell correctly.

Suggestion(s) for support

Those children who need support could, at the sorting stage, tick off on their list of words all the cards they already have. They could then play the game using the list only, so that they do not have to physically manipulate cards at the same time.

Assessment opportunities

Observation of children playing the game will enable teachers to note which children are familiar with the blend families involved.

After several opportunities have been given to play the game, groups could be given a spelling test on the words they have met.

Display ideas

Charts for each of the families could be made and displayed with a challenge such as 'Can you learn to spell 3 'st' words and 3 'sw' words this week? Tell me when you think you can spell 6 words and I will test you.'

Aspects of the English PoS covered

Writing – 2d.

98

SPELLING AND PHONICS KS1

PATTERNS

To focus on sets of words having the same letter patterns.

†† *Small group.*

🕐 *15–30 minutes, depending on the players' involvement, concentration and interest.*

Previous skills/knowledge needed

The game can be played at many levels depending on the observed needs of the children. For example, if children are at the very early stages of spelling phonically, sets of regular three-letter words could be used; if a group of children regularly misspell words with a particular pattern, sets of words incorporating that pattern could be used. Useful words are shown in the tables below.

Words with the same letter patterns

hat	cut	real	tore
mat	put	meal	core
sat	hut	seal	sore
cat	but	heal	more
set	read	bean	hope
pet	bead	mean	rope
get	dead	lean	mope
let	lead	jeans	Pope
sit	meat	bone	rose
hit	seat	gone	lose
bit	heat	done	hose
fit	beat	none	nose
not	hear	come	said
lot	dear	home	paid
hot	fear	some	laid
cot	bear	dome	raid

Words with commonly misspelled letter patterns

ight	*ough*	*ought*	*our*	*ie*
night	although	bought	our	pie
right	cough	brought	your	lie
fight	enough	ought	hour	piece
sight	rough	thought	flour	niece
fright	through	fought	pour	shield
might	tough		sour	thief
tight			course	field
bright			court	chief
light			fourteen	believe
delight			favourite	fierce
flight				frieze
				priest

Key background information

This activity focuses the children's attention on the *written* letter patterns at the point when the identification of sounds in words is proving to be unreliable. Children need to be made aware that the spelling of individual words does not always depend on direct letter–sound correspondence, and that they need to *look* for letter patterns in words. This kind of activity helps to reinforce the children's understanding that a spelling pattern does not consistently produce the same sound in spoken language.

Preparation

Prepare a set of cards, with four words in each set, for each player. This game can be played by any number of children, provided that there is a set of four cards for each player. Make another set of cards containing just the letter patterns you are using.

Resources needed

Sets of cards (see 'Preparation').

What to do

Shuffle the cards and deal out four to each player. The aim is to collect one set of words with the same letter pattern. Players look at their cards and place face down on the table one card which they do not want to keep. When everyone has decided on a card, the unwanted cards are slid, still face down, in a clockwise direction, to the next player. Each player then looks at the card they have been passed and decides whether they wish to keep it; if so, they pick it up and choose another card to pass on. If they do not wish to keep the card it is replaced, face down, on the table and passed on to the next player.

This process of discarding is repeated until one player has a complete set. As a variation, do not stop when one player has a set, but continue, with players dropping out as they complete a set, until every player has a full set.

SPELLING AND PHONICS KS1

WORDS INSIDE WORDS

To help children identify common letter strings/small words embedded in long words.

†† *Individual or small group.*

⏰ *15–30 minutes, depending on the level of involvement of the children.*

Previous skills/knowledge needed

Children will need some familiarity with the smaller words, so should therefore be able to read simple texts independently.

Key background information

This activity is often carried out as a short classroom activity, with the aim of finding as many words as possible using any letters from the given word in any order. This is enjoyable but does not necessarily help children to focus on letter patterns which will improve their spelling. This version of the activity does not ask children to find large numbers of words, because the letters have to be used in the same order as they appear in the original word.

Preparation

Collection of likely words for the game. The following list offers some useful ideas.

grandmother	– grand, and, moth, mother, other, the, her
interesting	– interest, in, rest, resting, tin, sting
justification	– just, if, cat, on, at, us
comfortable	– comfort, for, fort, tab, able, table, or
consideration	– consider, on, side, rat, ration, at
information	– in, for, form, mat, at, on
knowledgeable	– know, now, no, ledge, led, able, owl
mistletoe	– mist, is, let, to, toe

Suggestion(s) for extension

The game uses sets of only four words with the same pattern. Once the players appear familiar with the pattern(s) they could be asked to find other words with the same pattern.

Suggestion(s) for support

To begin with children could be given cards with just the letter patterns on them and use these to check words as they appear, for example '-at', '-one', -ight'.

If individual children find the game difficult they could play in pairs until they have gained confidence.

Assessment opportunities

After playing the game(s) children could be asked to write down as many words as they can remember for one or several of the letter patterns. This should reveal whether they have become familiar with the targeted pattern and a record can be made of those they know. After the activity their writing should be monitored to see whether the patterns are being used correctly; if errors continue to appear, they could be reminded of the pattern and, perhaps, play the game(s) again.

Display ideas

Charts of the letter-pattern sets can be made and two different ones displayed each week. Challenge the children to learn to spell one set in the week and test those who think they can spell them at the end of the week.

Aspects of the English PoS covered

Writing – 2d.

clambering	– clam, lamb, amber, am, ring, in
newspaper	– new, news, spa, paper, ape
overbearing	– over, verb, bear, ear, ring, in
priceless	– price, rice, ice, less

NB. Children's names and place-names are also excellent resources for this game.

Resources needed
Chalkboard and chalk, paper, writing materials, coloured felt-tipped pens or crayons.

What to do
Write a long word on the chalkboard and, if necessary, explain its meaning to the children. Explain that the aim is to find as many smaller words as possible within the given word and that the letters must be used in the same order as in the long word. Demonstrate with an example:
'disadvantage' = 'is', 'sad', 'van', 'ant', 'tag', 'age'.

'Can you find a two-letter word beginning with "i"? Can you find a three-letter word which is the opposite of "happy"? Can you find the name of a very small creature?'

Suggestion(s) for extension
Put a time-limit on the game: who can find the most words in 30 seconds or one minute?

Ask children to seek out words themselves which contain smaller words. They could then challenge their friends to find them all.

Suggestion(s) for support
Children who have difficulty locating the small words could be given a list of the words to look for and could then underline them in the longer word, using a different colour for each one.

Assessment opportunities
Observation of the children working and of their responses to the challenge to find long words with little ones inside could provide detail for teachers' ongoing records. Notes can be made about whether individuals are developing the ability both to locate and to use particular letter strings in their own writing.

Display ideas
A display could be made of all the long words used, shown in order, for example:

▲ Alice = ice (1 word)
▲ between = bet, we (2 words)
▲ content = ten, tent, on (3 words)

This could become an ongoing class challenge to see who can find words that have more small words than any others so far!

Aspects of the English PoS covered
Writing – 2d.

LETTER STRING CHALLENGE

To focus on sets of words having the same letter patterns.

†† *Pairs, either challenged by the teacher or challenging each other.*

🕐 *15–20 minutes, depending on the players' enthusiasm and concentration.*

Previous skills/knowledge needed
Children will need to have done some previous work focusing on letter patterns. The teacher could select particular patterns or letter strings which individual players need to practise. Alternatively, children could choose patterns or letter strings for themselves that they think they know in order to challenge each other.

Key background information
The activity is intended to reinforce the visual recall of particular common letter strings. Children need to be encouraged to become so familiar with these that the writing of them is automatic.

Preparation
Decide which letter strings you wish to concentrate on and write them on a set of cards. A list of common letter strings is given overleaf. Copy the 'Game record sheet' from photocopiable page 150 for each child.

Graphic knowledge

Common letter strings

-ang	-ash	-ough	-ing	-tch
-amp	-ate	-ore	-ie	-con
-air	-are	-ool	-ion	-dge
-all	-art	-ead	-ind	-man
-ain	-ame	-each	-ine	-the
-and	-ack	-end	-ign	-tion
-ast	-our	-ear	-ice	-whe
-age	-ong	-ent	-ide	-her
-ail	-ould	-ell	-ill	-per
-aid	-oat	-eat	-igh	-str
-ace	-out	-ease	-ite	-com
-ank	-oin	-eel	-ure	-ly
-ate	-one	-est	-use	-squ

Resources needed

Letter string cards (see 'Preparation'), a timer (sand-glass or clock), 'Game record sheet' on photocopiable page 150 for each child, writing materials.

What to do

Explain to the children that they are going to be given a letter string. Tell them that they will then have to write down as many words as they can think of containing that pattern. The pattern can be used in any part of the word. Explain that, to make it more exciting, they will only have a limited amount of time and they will be competing to see who can come up with the most words.

Give each child one card with a letter string written on it. Then give each child a 'Game record sheet' for them to write their answers on. When both players are ready, the cards are turned over and the timer started. If a sand-glass is used, the time allowed will be predetermined, but a clock timer can be set for any given time. Initially, if possible, a longer time should be allowed and this can be decreased to make the challenge more difficult and exciting when the players are more familiar with the letters being used.

At the end of the given time the words are counted up and the winner is the player with the most *correctly spelled* words using their own letter pattern. Nonsense words do not count only real words are allowed.

Suggestion(s) for extension

This challenge can be adapted easily to meet the needs of the children and the intentions of the teacher. The difficulty of the task depends on the letter strings selected and the time allowed for writing the words. Once they are familiar with the game, children should be invited to challenge each other with particular letter strings.

Suggestion(s) for support

The game could be introduced as a self-challenge for children who think they have learned a particular pattern. They should try writing down as many words as they can remember, using the chosen letter string, before the timer runs out.

For the least confident children the challenge could be undertaken in pairs, that is one pair challenges another pair.

Assessment opportunities

Record sheets from photocopiable page xxx can be retained by the teacher as a record of the letter strings each child knows well and as indicators of where further practice might be needed. The 'Graphic knowledge assessment sheet' on photocopiable page 151 can be used to assess children's growing knowledge of common spelling patterns.

Display ideas

Create a 'Spelling Board' display, headed 'We can spell all these words'. Children can put up their own lists with headings such as, 'Peter can spell all these words'. The children could add a list whenever they have learned a new set of words. Change the lists regularly.

Aspects of the English PoS covered

Writing – 2d.

Reference to photocopiable sheets

Photocopiable page 150 contains a record sheet on which children should write down all the words they think of. This can be attached to the 'Graphic knowledge assessment sheet' on photocopiable page 151.

'AND' AND 'ING' PELMANISM

To familiarise children with common letter patterns.
To enable children to focus on consistent letter strings.

†† *Small group of 2–5.*

🕐 *15–30 minutes, depending on the players' interest and concentration.*

Previous skills/knowledge needed

Children should have been introduced to the two letter strings 'and' and 'ing', possibly through a shared reading activity where the letter combinations have been pointed out by the teacher. Similarly, the patterns could have been commented on during a shared writing session with a larger group, or in a child's own writing.

Key background information

The letter strings 'and' and 'ing' are among the earliest which children notice and it is always helpful, in teaching about letters and how they fit together in writing, to capitalise on what the children are already aware of. Some children do not naturally notice patterns in words and it is particularly important for these children to help them focus on visual patterns as soon as possible. This game can be played with any sets of words having common letter strings, but this version focuses on familiarising children with these two common patterns.

Preparation

Prepare and laminate a set of cards with a variety of words incorporating the letter strings 'and' and 'ing' (see table for suggested words). There must be an even number of words because they are to be paired. Make a further set of these cards with the letter strings underlined for the support activity.

Words containing 'and' and 'ing'

and	dandelion	swing
sand	handle	king
band	land	ring
hand	sandal	thing
stand	sandwich	nothing
Andrew	wander	dining-room
Sandra (plus	island	doing
any other	England	ending
names present	sing	evening
in the class)	bring	finger
handstand	string	single
candle	jingle	spring
panda	going	wedding

Resources needed

Set of letter string word cards (see 'Preparation').

What to do

Explain to the players that all the cards contain words with either 'and' or 'ing' in them, and that the aim is to collect as many pairs of 'and' or 'ing' words as possible.

Start the game by laying all the cards out randomly, face down on the table.

The first player turns over one card and says whether there is an 'and' or an 'ing' in the word, reading the word aloud if possible. Any player can read the word. A second card is turned over and, if it is a word with the same letter pattern, the player takes both cards. If it is a word with the other letter pattern, both cards are returned to the face-down position. If a player succeeds in taking a pair of cards, he has another turn.

The next player repeats the procedure. All players should try to remember the positions of particular words, so that they can judge better which ones to turn over in the future.

The game continues until all the cards have been picked up. The winner is the player with the most pairs of words.

Suggestion(s) for extension

When all the cards have been paired, the more confident children could be asked to read aloud all the words that they have collected.

Children who are confident in identifying these letter patterns could make another version of the game using another two common letter strings.

Suggestion(s) for support

If individual children have difficulty in spotting the patterns, they could use a set of cards with the letter strings underlined so that they are easier to spot. After a few games with this version, they could move on to the version described in the main activity, without the underlinings.

Assessment opportunities

It is important that teachers are aware of which children can confidently identify common letter strings. For those who cannot, the teacher will need to provide as many opportunities as possible to draw the children's attention to the common ones. Observation of children playing this game and/or a conversation with them, asking them to point out the letters, will enable the teacher to record whether an individual is confident or not.

Display ideas

After playing the game children could be asked to write down all the 'and' or 'ing' words they can spell and their lists could be added to a wall display of 'Words we can spell' (see also Display ideas for 'Letter string challenge').

Aspects of the English PoS covered

Writing – 2d.

VERB SUFFIXES PELMANISM

To introduce the term 'suffix'. To familiarise children with the common tense marker suffixes.

†† *Small group.*

🕐 *15–30 minutes, depending on the players' level of interest.*

Previous skills/knowledge needed

Children should have some experience of looking at syllables in words, which may well have raised issues about the consistent appearance of common verb endings.

Key background information

Verb ending suffixes are relatively consistent in regular verbs and familiarity with these endings helps to ensure their correct spelling. For this game, words have been selected which do not need to have letters changed or omitted for the addition of the suffix. Many verbs do require such changes, but this issue is best dealt with once children are familiar with the suffix/ending. Children may notice that these verb roots all end with a consonant.

Preparation

Copy the verb roots on photocopiable page 152 twice and page 153 once directly on to card or mount copies on to card. Copy photocopiable page 154 on to a different-coloured sheet of card. You will need to copy this page three times so that you have enough suffixes for all the verb roots. Laminate the cards and cut them up as indicated. Provide a container for storage.

Resources needed

A set of root and suffix cards (see 'Preparation'), booklets, writing materials.

What to do

Spread out all the cards face down on a table. Show the children how to play the game by turning over two cards – one of each colour. Put the two cards together and read out the resulting word. Explain that if they are a root and a suffix which match appropriately (for example, 'talk' and '-ed') the two parts should both be removed; if the two parts do not match appropriately (for example, 'buy' and '-ed') the cards should be replaced face down on the table. The game continues in this way, with players taking each matched pair they turn up, until all the cards have been removed. The players should be warned that there will be some pairs which do not match and that they should try the word out before removing the cards. The winner is the player with the most correct pairs of cards. If there are any cards left over, each player's cards should be checked to find the non-words (for example, 'bring' + '-ed').

SPELLING AND
PHONICS KS1

Graphic knowledge

Suggestion(s) for extension

Challenge those children who complete the game easily to find more words which can take *both* '-ed' and '-ing' suffixes without any changes to the root. There are a great many such verbs. This could be further extended by a further challenge to find ones which have irregular past tenses.

Suggestion(s) for support

Some children may be very unsure about the '-ed' suffix and may be prepared to accept 'bringed' or 'buyed'. This would be the starting point for further discussion about the irregular past tenses of verbs such as 'bring' or 'buy'. They could make personal collections (in made-up booklets) of all the verbs they can find with irregular endings.

Assessment opportunities

This game will show whether individuals are able to identify the two suffixes focused on and whether they understand that these have a constant spelling pattern even if the pronunciation seems to suggest otherwise (for example, 'walked' not 'walk'). When understanding of this is secure, further work may need to be done on those roots which require changes before the addition of the suffix (for example, those ending in 'e' such as 'like'). This activity may reveal that some children are using non-standard forms of the past tense in their spoken language; a note should be made of this so that further work can be planned to develop familiarity with the written forms of the past tense in standard English. Correction of non-standard forms in spoken language needs sensitivity.

Opportunities for IT

Children could use a hand-held electronic thesaurus or a spelling checker from a word processor to check the spellings of some of the words they have created, especially if they are unsure about the validity of a particular word. This would be most easily achieved if the children typed the words they have made on to a word processor so that they could use the spelling checker. This list could also act as a record of the children's work for assessment purposes.

Display ideas

After the game has been played by several groups of children, make a display headed 'Verbs – spelling the past tense'. Start this off by writing one or two regular verbs thus: play – play<u>ed</u>, laugh – laugh<u>ed</u>. Ask the children to add regular past tense verbs to the list. When this is quite long, make a second display of 'Verbs – irregular past tenses'. Start it off thus: buy – bought, say – said, and ask the children to add others they know.

This display will need to be explained to the children, particularly the terminology used that is verb, tense, past, regular, irregular.

Aspects of the English PoS covered

Reading – 2b.

Reference to photocopiable sheets

Photocopiable page 152 contains 18 regular verb roots. Photocopiable page 153 contains 18 irregular verb roots. Photocopiable page 154 contains the verb suffixes '-ed' and '-ing'. To play 'Verb suffixes Pelmanism' you will need two copies of page 152, one copy of page 153 and three copies of page 154 to ensure that all the cards can be matched up.

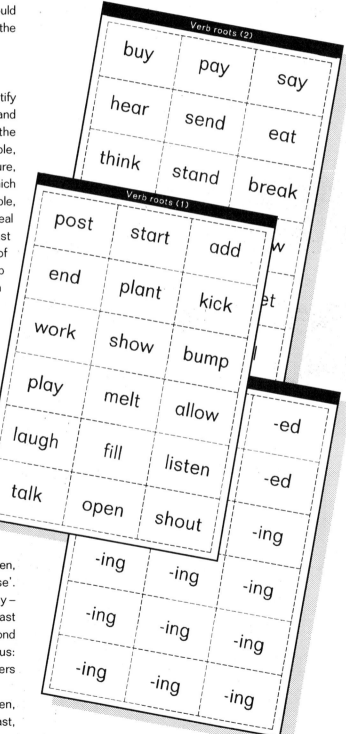

FIXING OPPOSITES

To introduce the term 'prefix'. To focus on the meanings of the common prefixes – 'un' and 'dis'.

†† *Pairs.*

🕒 *15–20 minutes.*

Previous skills/knowledge needed

Children should have looked at syllables in words, which may well have raised issues about the consistent appearance of common prefixes. The starting point for discussion of prefixes should be words familiar to the children, such as 'unhappy' or 'disagree'.

Key background information

A prefix is a group of letters placed at the beginning of a word to change or extend its meaning. It sometimes happens that a word with a prefix has a very different meaning from the word without the prefix (for example, 'compose'/ 'decompose'), but most have a consistent meaning and many will create a new word which has an opposite meaning. This is a fairly complex area for young children and it is better to concentrate on very common, familiar words. Some words can have more than one prefix added to them to make new words with different meanings. In this game, for example, 'able' can become 'unable' or 'disable'. The differences in the resulting words should be discussed with the children.

Preparation

Copy the words and prefixes on photocopiable page 155 on to card or mount copies on to card. If possible, laminate the

cards to make them more durable. Mark the two prefix cards in some way to make them stand out from the rest. You will have to make one set for each pair of children undertaking the activity. Copy 'Opposites record sheet (1)' on photocopiable page 156 for each child. Copy 'Opposites record sheet (2)' on photocopiable page 157 for each child undertaking the support activity.

Resources needed

Sets of cards and record sheets (see 'Preparation'), writing materials.

What to do

Give each pair of children a set of the cards and tell them to spread them out on a table so that all the cards can be seen. Point out the two prefixes 'un' and 'dis' and explain that these can be added to the other words in the set to make words which have the opposite meaning. Explain that 'un' and 'dis' mean 'not'. Show the children how to put together a prefix card and a word card to make an opposite, for example 'un' + 'happy'. Give each child an 'Opposites record sheet' and ask them to write the original word and its newly-created opposite under the appropriate headings, and then to write what the opposite means in the third column as shown in the illustration.

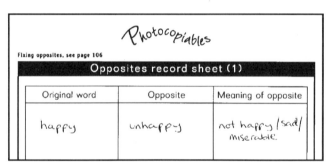

Photocopiables

Fixing opposites, see page 106

Opposites record sheet (1)

Original word	Opposite	Meaning of opposite
happy	unhappy	not happy / sad / miserable

The children should then continue to try each prefix with each word, decide which one is appropriate to make the opposite (NB In the case of 'able', both 'un' and 'dis' make acceptable opposites) and then write down the words as in the example.

When the pair have finished sorting the words, they should compare their list with another pair and see whether they agree. Disagreements should be discussed and a decision made about which suggestion is correct. The lists should then be discussed with the teacher.

Suggestion(s) for extension

Children who cope easily with this activity could be asked to make up some nonsense opposites of their own, using the prefixes 'un' and 'dis', for example 'unbig' or 'unopen'. This kind of activity, playing with words, is not only enjoyable but also reinforces the concept of prefixes being additions to words.

Graphic Knowledge

Suggestion(s) for support
Where children have difficulty deciding which prefix would be appropriate for particular words, they should be given one prefix only, together with the set of words which can be used with that prefix. They should then complete 'Opposites record sheet (2)' as shown in the illustration.

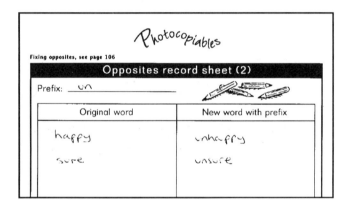

Assessment opportunities
Note whether the children have understood the concept of a prefix. The record sheets could be retained as a record of each child's understanding of the words.

Opportunities for IT
Children could use a hand-held electronic thesaurus or a spelling checker from a word processor to check the spellings of some of the words they have created, especially if they are unsure about the validity of a particular word. This would be most easily achieved if the children typed the words they have made on to a word processor so that they could use the spelling checker. The typed list could also serve as a record of the children's work for assessment purposes.

Display ideas
Display heading 'Making opposites'. Make a display using all the words in this game, written up in the same way as on the children's worksheet, that is: word – opposite – meaning.

Ask the children to add to the list any other opposites they know using the prefixes 'un' or 'dis'.

Aspects of the English PoS covered
Reading – 2b.

Reference to photocopiable sheets
Use photocopiable page 155 to make individual cards of words and prefixes. Photocopiable pages 156 and 157 offer sheets for the children to record the new words they make (and their meanings).

Glossary

GLOSSARY OF ESSENTIAL TERMS

Alliteration	a sequence of words beginning with the same sound.	**Onset and rime**	'onset' is the consonant or cluster of consonants at the beginning of a word or syllable and 'rime' is the rest of the word or syllable, which enables the word to rhyme with other words.
Compound words	two or more words that combine to form a new word.		
Consonants	all the letters of the alphabet except the vowels.	**Phoneme**	the smallest unit of sound that can be spoken or heard, such as 'c' as in 'cat'. Over 44 vowel and consonant sounds have been identified in English.
Consonant digraphs	two consonants which combine to make a new sound, such as 'ch', 'sh', 'wh', 'th', 'ph', 'gh', 'ng'.		
Diphthong	two vowels sounds that combine together to make a single new sound within a syllable. The mouth changes position during the sounding process, for example, 'oil', 'toy', 'they', 'out', 'cow' and 'few' ('w' functions as a vowel).	**Phonic knowledge**	'the relationships between print symbol and sound patterns' (*English in the National Curriculum*, DFE, 1995).
		Polysyllabic	a word which has more than one syllable, such as 'alligator'.
		Prefixes	an affix at the beginning of a word, for example, 'disappoint', 'unhappy', 'redo'.
Doubled consonants	two identical consonants making the sound of one consonant, for example, 'bb', 'dd', 'ff'.	**Short vowel sounds**	For example in 'apple' (initial sound or as in 'cat' (middle sound).
Final consonant	a consonant which ends a word, for example, 'bag'.	**Silent letters**	these can occur at the beginning, end or middle of words, for example, 'b', 'g', 'gh', 'k'. 'E' is frequently silent at the end of words, for example, 'kettle'. Examples of silent letters include: 'through', 'crumb', 'knee', 'wrist', 'calm', 'sign', 'psalm'.
Grapheme	the smallest unit of sound represented as a written symbol. The 26 letters of the alphabet are graphemes. By changing a grapheme in a word it is possible to change the meaning as in [c]at to [b]at.		
		Suffixes	an affix at the end of a word, for example, 'wanted', 'useful', 'alliteration'.
Graphic knowledge	'what can be learned about word meanings and parts of words from consistent letter patterns' (*English in the National Curriculum*, DFE., 1995).	**Syllable**	a rhythmic segment of a word, spoken or written which consists of a combination of vowel(s) plus consonant(s) or consonant(s) plus vowel(s).
Initial consonant	a consonant which begins a word, for example, boy.		
Initial consonant blends	the consonants retain their original sounds but run or are 'blended' together. For example, 'bl', 'br', 'cl', 'dr', 'pl', 'fr'.	**Triple consonants**	three letter 'blends', for example, 'str', 'spr'.
		Vowels	'a', 'e', 'i', 'o', 'u'. The letter 'y' can also function as a vowel, as in 'ay', 'ey', 'iy', 'oy', 'uy'. 'Y' also functions as a vowel in unusual words such as 'rhythm'.
Long vowel sounds	For example, as in 'late'.		
Metalanguage	a language with which to talk about language. Children need to meet essential terminology in order to help them talk about words.	**Vowel digraph**	a combination of two symbols that represent sound unlike that of either of the individual letters. When a digraph is sounded the shape of the mouth does not change during the sounding process. Examples of vowel digraphs include: 'ai', 'ay', 'ee', 'ie', 'oa', 'oe', 'au'.
Monosyllabic	a word of one syllable, for example 'dog'.		

108

SPELLING AND
PHONICS KS1

Photocopiables

The pages in this section can be photocopied for use in the classroom or school which has purchased this book, and do not need to be declared in any return in respect of any photocopying licence.

They comprise a varied selection of both pupil and teacher resources, including pupil worksheets, resource material and record sheets to be completed by the teacher or children. Most of the photocopiable pages are related to individual activities in the book; the name of the activity is indicated at the top of the sheet, together with a page reference indicating where the lesson plan for that activity can be found.

Individual pages are discussed in detail within each lesson plan, accompanied by ideas for adaptation where appropriate – of course, each sheet can be adapted to your own needs and those of your class. Sheets can also be coloured, laminated, mounted on to card, enlarged and so on where appropriate.

Pupil worksheets and record sheets have spaces provided for children's names and for noting the date on which each sheet was used. This means that, if so required, they can be included easily within any pupil assessment portfolio.

'I Spy', see page 20

Initial and final sounds assessment sheet

Name:	Age:	Date:

Languages spoken:	

Comment on the child's ability to:	
▲ identify initial sound of own name.	
▲ identify final sound of own name.	
▲ identify initial sound of others' names.	
▲ identify final sound of others' names.	
▲ identify initial sound of a range of items.	
▲ identify final sound of a range of items.	
▲ identify differences between the initial sounds of names that sound the same but are spelled differently (eg. *Philip* and *Fred*).	
▲ identify initial single consonants.	
▲ identify initial vowels.	
▲ identify initial consonant blends.	
▲ identify initial consonant digraphs.	
Errors/confusions:	
Other comments:	

SPELLING AND
PHONICS KS1

Photocopiables

'I Spy' kitchen game, see page 20

Kitchen game cards

SPELLING AND
PHONICS KS1

'I Spy' kitchen game, see page 20

Kitchen game cards

'I Spy' kitchen game, see page 20

Alphabet knowledge record sheet

Name:	Age:	Date:

Languages spoken:

Comments on individual letters:

Comment on the child's ability to:

▲ link initial letter sounds to a familiar set of objects.	
▲ link printed initial letter sounds cards to a familiar set of objects.	
▲ sort set of objects into alphabetical order.	
▲ sort alphabet cards into alphabetical order.	

Errors/confusions:

Other comments:

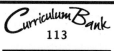

**SPELLING AND
PHONICS KS1**

Photocopiables

Card templates

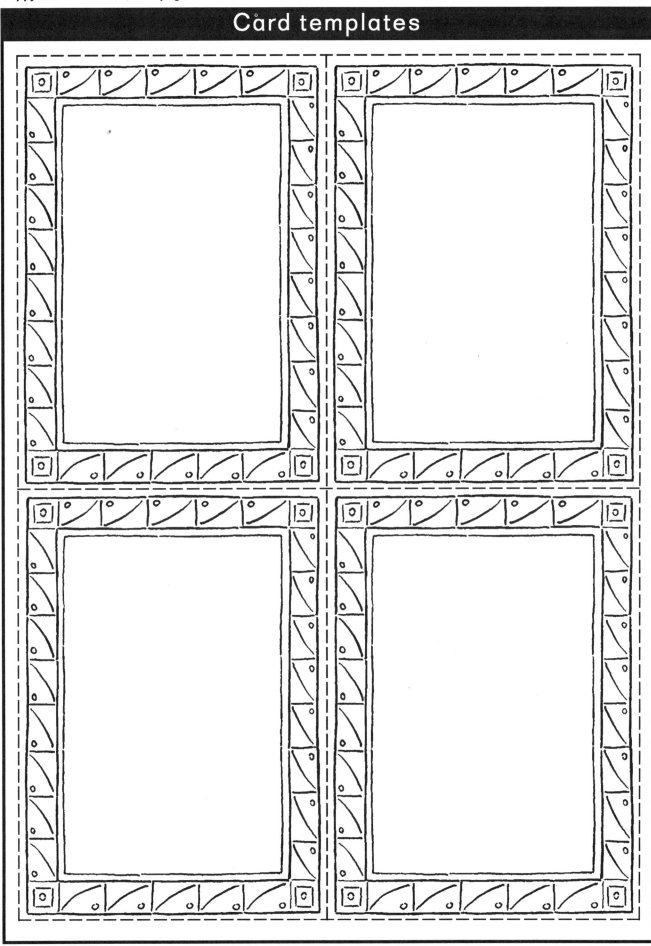

SPELLING AND PHONICS KS1

Happy name families: assessment sheet

Name:	Age:	Date:

Comment on the child's ability to:

▲ recognise own name.	
▲ recognise initial sound of name.	
▲ recognises final sound of name.	
▲ recognise other names in own Happy Name Family.	
▲ recognise other name families.	
▲ recognise initial sounds in other names.	
▲ recognise final sounds in other names.	
▲ recognise other sounds/ combinations of letters.	
▲ demonstrate knowledge of alphabet (list letters).	
▲ demonstrate knowledge of alphabetical order.	
▲ place own/others' names at the beginning/middle/end of alphabet.	

Other observations:

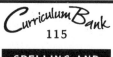

SPELLING AND PHONICS KS1

'I Spy' word chain, see page 34

'I Spy' word chain: assessment sheet

Name:	Age: Date(s):

Languages spoken:

Comment on the child's ability to:

▲ identify objects by initial sound.	
▲ identify final sound in words.	
▲ use initial single consonants.	
▲ use initial vowel sounds (short).	
▲ use initial vowel sounds (long).	
▲ use initial consonant digraphs.	
▲ use initial consonant blends.	
▲ use final and silent 'e'.	
▲ use silent letters.	

Other observations:
Areas of difficulty:
Further comments/future experience needed:

SPELLING AND PHONICS KS1

Word chain card game: record sheet

Date:		
Word	Child's name	Observations

117

One word ABC, see page 41

Alphabet record sheet: writing

Name:	Age:	Date:

Languages spoken:

Comment on:

▲ the child's growing knowledge of writing the alphabet in sequence.	
▲ the child's development in letter formation.	
▲ gaps in the child's knowledge of writing the alphabet.	
▲ the child's level of independence, eg. using displays, dictionaries, etc.	
▲ areas of confusion/errors.	

General comments on individual letters:

SPELLING AND PHONICS KS1

Tidy the library, see page 46

Bookshelf

**SPELLING AND
PHONICS KS1**

Tidy the library, see page 46

Library books (1)

▲ The library has been left in a terrible mess. Someone has left books all over the floor. Can you clear it up and put all the books back on to the bookshelf?

Cut the books out and stick them back on the shelf. Don't forget the books must go back in alphabetical order.

J. & A. Ahlberg

P. Hutchins

A. Brown

J. Kerr

R. Dahl

E.B. White

E. Carle

R. Maris

M. Sendak

▲ Use the alphabet below to help you.

A B C D E F G H I J K L M N O P Q R S T U V W X Y Z

Curriculum Bank
120

SPELLING AND
PHONICS KS1

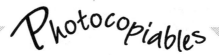

Tidy the library, see page 46

Library books (2)

▲ The library has been left in a terrible mess with books lying all over the floor. Can you tidy it up? Think carefully about the two books whose authors' names start with the same letter.

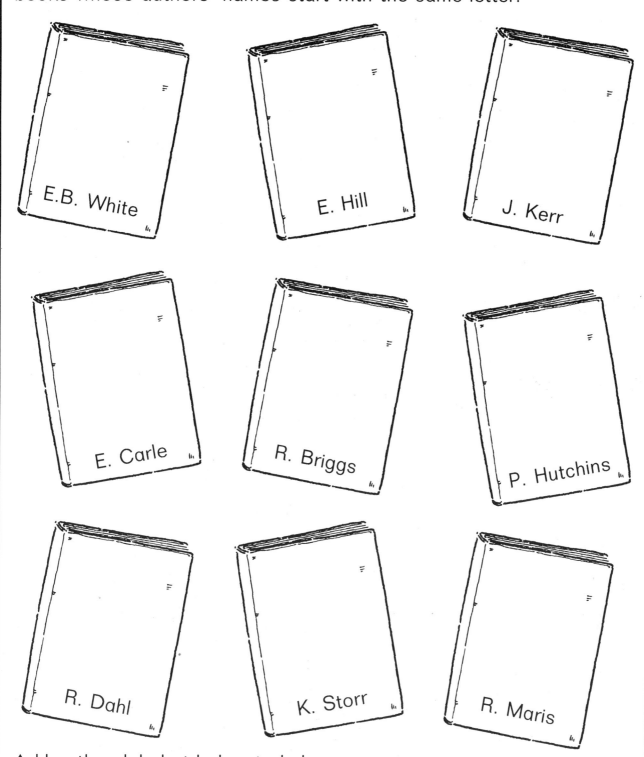

E.B. White

E. Hill

J. Kerr

E. Carle

R. Briggs

P. Hutchins

R. Dahl

K. Storr

R. Maris

▲ Use the alphabet below to help you.

A B C D E F G H I J K L M N O P Q R S T U V W X Y Z

SPELLING AND
PHONICS KS1

Tidy the library, see page 46

Library books (3)

▲ The library has been left in a terrible mess. Can you tidy it up and put all the books back on the shelf?

Cut the books out and stick them back on the shelf. The books must go back in alphabetical order.

▲ Use the alphabet below to help you.

A B C D E F G H I J K L M N O P Q R S T U V W X Y Z

'Humpty Dumpty' listening for rhymes, see page 50

Humpty Dumpty

Humpty Dumpty sat on a wall,
Humpty Dumpty had a great fall;
All the king's horses and all the king's men
Couldn't put Humpty together again.

One, two, buckle my shoe

One, two
Buckle my shoe.
Three, four
Knock at the door.
Five, six
Pick up sticks
Seven, eight
Lay them straight.
Nine, ten
A big fat hen.

Eleven, twelve
Dig and delve.
Thirteen, fourteen
Maids a-courting.
Fifteen, sixteen
Maids in the kitchen.
Seventeen, eighteen
Maids a-waiting.
Nineteen, twenty
My plate's empty.

Little Jack Horner

Little Jack Horner
Sat in the corner,
Eating a Christmas pie;
He put in his thumb,
And pulled out a plum,
And said, 'What a good boy am I.'

One, two, three, four, five

One, two, three, four, five,
Once I caught a fish alive.
Six, seven, eight, nine, ten,
Then I let it go again.

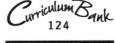

'Humpty Dumpty' listening for rhymes, see page 50

Growing awareness of rhyme: assessment sheet 1

Name:	Age:	Date:

Languages spoken:	

Comment on:	
▲ the child's knowledge of nursery rhymes and/or other rhymes.	
▲ the child's growing understanding of the word 'rhyme'.	
▲ the child's awareness of rhymes in 'Humpty Dumpty' (or other rhymes).	
▲ pairs of rhymes the child successfully identified.	
▲ whether the child could identify the part of the words that rhymed.	
▲ whether the child could suggest words to build rhyme families.	
▲ whether the child could see different rhyme patterns in more complex nursery rhymes.	
▲ whether the child noticed the change that is achieved in words by altering the initial sound (phoneme).	
▲ whether the child systematically ran through possible phonemes alphabetically, in order to create new rhyming words.	
▲ areas of particular difficulty or lack of sensitivity to rhyme.	

SPELLING AND PHONICS KS1

'Humpty Dumpty' looking for rhymes, see page 52

How well does it rhyme? (1)

▲ Working with a partner, read the rhyme through. Listen carefully for the rhymes.

One, two, three, four, five,
Once I caught a fish alive.
Six, seven, eight, nine, ten,
Then I let it go again.

▲ There are four rhyming words. Can you find them? Put a circle round the words.

▲ Now, write the rhyming words. The rhyming words are:

1 _____

2 _____

3 _____

4 _____

▲ Two words have their rhyme spelled the same way. Write down the two words.

1 _____

2 _____

▲ Find the two rhyming words that are spelled in different ways. Write them down.

1 _____

2 _____

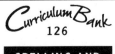

'Humpty Dumpty' looking for rhymes, see page 52

How well does it rhyme? (2)

▲ Look at the poem, 'One, two, buckle my shoe', then answer these questions.

▲ Draw a line underneath all the rhyming words.

▲ Find a pair of rhyming words that rhyme exactly and have the same spelling pattern. Write the words on the lines below.

1 _____

2 _____

▲ Find a pair of words that rhyme but have different spelling patterns. Write the words on the lines below.

1 _____

2 _____

▲ Find a pair of words that don't quite rhyme. Write the words on the lines below. One pair has already been done.

1. fourteen   2. _____

   a-courting   _____

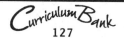
127

SPELLING AND
PHONICS KS1

'Humpty Dumpty' looking for rhymes, see page 52

Growing awareness of rhyme: assessment sheet 2

Name:	Age:	Date:

Languages spoken:		

When the child looks at the structure of rhyme families do they comment on:

▲ changes in graphemes?	
▲ the constancy of rhymes?	
▲ the patterns of letters in rhymes?	
▲ the fact that not all rhymes are spelled in precisely the same way (eg. 'eight' and 'straight')?	
▲ other similarities and differences?	

When constructing rhyme families does the child:

▲ try all possible combinations including nonsense words?	
▲ use classroom resources, eg. dictionaries?	
▲ list the rhyme family by making mental substitutions?	
▲ notice when rhymes are not quite an exact match?	

Other comments:

**SPELLING AND
PHONICS KS1**

'Lucky dip' a rhyming game, see page 54

Picture clue cards

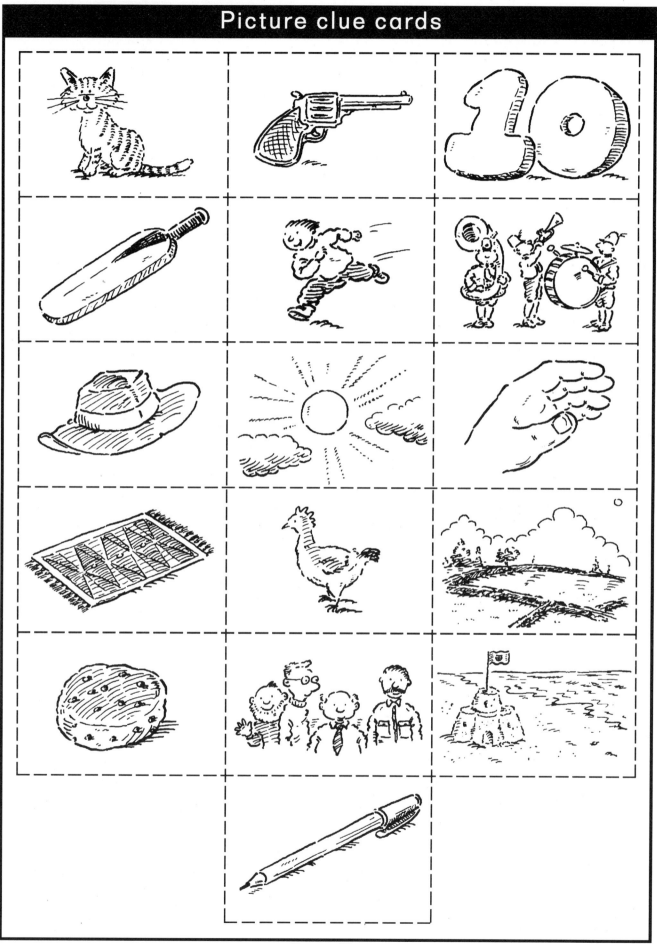

SPELLING AND
PHONICS KS1

Odd one out (1), see page 56

Rhyme pack (1)

cat	mat	hen
bat	pat	dog
hat	rat	egg
fat	sat	pig

Rhyme pack (2)

neat	seat	moon
meat	beat	sing
treat	repeat	keep
eat	heat	fun

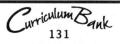

Odd one out (1), see page 56

Alliteration pack

cup	carrot	bag
cot	coat	pig
cap	car	dog
cake	cat	goat

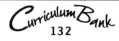

SPELLING AND
PHONICS KS1

Rhyme family cards (1)

cat	gun	pot
bat	run	big
hat	sun	dig
fat	cot	fig
bun	dot	pig

hot

SPELLING AND
PHONICS KS1

Odd one out (2), see page 59

Rhyme family cards (2)

book	heat	sing
cook	meat	best
hook	seat	nest
rook	bring	rest
eat	king	vest
	ring	

SPELLING AND
PHONICS KS1

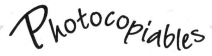

Creating tongue twisters, see page 66

Peter Piper

Peter Piper picked a peck of pickled pepper.
If Peter Piper picked a peck of pickled pepper,
Where's the peck of pickled pepper
Peter Piper picked?

She sells sea shells

She sells sea shells
By the sea shore.
The shells that she sells
Are sea shells, I'm sure.

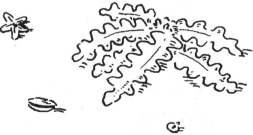

SPELLING AND
PHONICS KS1

Creating tongue twisters, see page 66

Betty Botter

Betty Botter bought some butter
But the butter Betty bought was bitter.
So Betty Botter bought some better butter,
Better than the bitter butter
Betty bought before.

Moses' toeses

Moses supposes his toeses are roses
But Moses supposes erroneously.
For nobody's toeses are posies of roses
As Moses supposes his toeses to be.

Clapping rhymes, see page 72

Jack and Jill

Jack and Jill went up the hill
To fetch a pail of water.
Jack fell down and broke his crown
And Jill came tumbling after.

Ten fat sausages

Ten fat sausages sizzling in the pan.
Ten fat sausages sizzling in the pan.
One went POP and the other went BANG!
There'll be eight fat sausages sizzling in the pan.

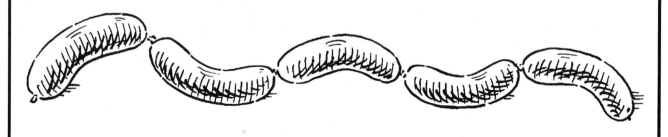

Clapping rhymes, see page 72

Counting claps (1)

▲ Read 'Jack and Jill' out loud. As you do so, clap the rhythm.

Jack and Jill went up the hill
To fetch a pail of water.
Jack fell down and broke his crown
And Jill came tumbling after.

▲ Now answer these questions:

Write *three* words which have only one clap:

1. _____

2. _____

3. _____

Write *two* words which have two claps:

1. _____

2. _____

How many claps can you count in the whole rhyme?

I can count _____ claps in 'Jack and Jill'.

SPELLING AND PHONICS KS1

Clapping rhymes, see page 72

Counting claps (2)

▲ Read 'Ten fat sausages' out loud. As you do so, clap the rhythm.

Ten fat sausages sizzling in the pan.
Ten fat sausages sizzling in the pan.
One went POP and the other went BANG!
There'll be eight fat sausages sizzling in the pan.

▲ Now answer these questions:

Write *two* words which have two claps:

1. _____

2. _____

Write *three* words which have one clap:

1. _____

2. _____

3. _____

How many claps can you count in the whole rhyme?

I can count _____ claps in 'Ten fat sausages'.

SPELLING AND
PHONICS KS1

Sorting out names, see page 75

How many syllables?

▲ On the lines below make a list of names. The list can include people in your family as well as your friends.

My list of names:

_____   _____

_____   _____   _____

_____   _____   _____

_____   _____   _____

▲ Now, look at your list of names and sort them into the syllable sets below. One name has been put into each set to start you off. My list of names sorted into syllable sets:

One-syllable names
John
_____

_____

_____

Three-syllable names
Jamila
_____

_____

_____

Two-syllable names
Lauren
_____

_____

_____

Four-syllable names
Sebastian
_____

_____

_____

Sorting out names, see page 75

Syllables assessment sheet

Name:	Age: Date:
Languages spoken:	

Comment on the child's ability to:

▲ clap with accuracy the rhythm of well-known rhymes.	
▲ identify well-known rhymes by listening to the rhythm.	
▲ clap the rhythm of people's names and other well-known words.	
▲ categorise names or well-known words by similarities and differences in the number of claps.	
▲ use the word 'syllable'.	
▲ identify the number of syllables in a range of polysyllabic words.	
▲ comment on the syllabic structure of compound words.	
▲ 'chunk' syllables.	
▲ comment on vowels in polysyllabic words.	
▲ comment on beginning, middle and end syllables.	
▲ manage syllables in his or her written language.	
Other comments:	

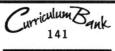

Seaside suitcase, see page 79

Seaside suitcase resource sheet

The bare bones of the 'Seaside Suitcase' story are printed in bold type. There are lists of compound words throughout the story for you to choose to include in this activity. The list is extensive and you will have to be very selective.

Once upon a time I went abroad for a holiday. In my suitcase I packed:
my passport

I needed some things for the beach:
a sundress
a swimsuit
a sunhat
a headscarf
and
a beachball

I also needed some sport items:
a sweatshirt
a tracksuit
a football
trainers
and, just in case,
a shoelace

And in case it rained I packed myself:
a raincoat
and
a rainhat

To keep myself amused I took:
my walkman
a crossword
and
a jigsaw

On the beach I built:
a sandcastle
but I couldn't bring it home, so I took
a snapshot

I also needed:
a rucksack
and
a handbag

which had in it:
a hairbrush
a hairgrip
lipstick
earrings
and
a necklace

In case I felt hungry I took some food:
a milkshake
a teabag
and some
popcorn
I took my own:
teacup
teaspoon
and
teapot

On the beach I collected:
a seahorse
a seashell
seaweed
and
a starfish

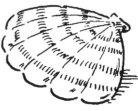

And at bedtime I needed:
toothpaste
my toothbrush
a nightdress/a nightshirt
and
bedsocks

Oh, I nearly forgot, before I came home I sent:
a postcard

At the end of my holiday, I had to pack everything back into my suitcase again!

Seaside suitcase, see page 79

Compound words

▲ Decide where these words split then illustrate one half of each word while your partner illustrates the other half.

bookcase

bookworm

moonlight

sunbeam

lunchtime

lighthouse

treehouse

SPELLING AND
PHONICS KS1

Seaside suitcase: spelling, see page 81

Can you pack the seaside suitcase? (1)

▲ The seaside suitcase needs packing. Each item in the suitcase has the second part of its luggage label missing. All the words you need to complete the labels are on the accompanying page. Cut out the words and stick them in the right places. The first label has been done for you.

Seaside suitcase: spelling, see page 81

Can you pack the seaside suitcase? (2)

▲ Cut out these words to complete the luggage labels.

fish

paste

ball

brush

shake

lace

card

man

brush

port

bag

horse

SPELLING AND
PHONICS KS1

Polysyllabic creatures, see page 83

Creature cards

antelope	dinosaur	nightingale
buffalo	elephant	octopus
butterfly	gorilla	parakeet
centipede	kangaroo	pelican
crocodile	Labrador	porcupine
chimpanzee	mosquito	unicorn

Haiku, see page 89

Haiku poems

▲ This poem is a haiku:

Sharp claws, bright green eyes
You catch birds in your strong jaws
Purring you sleep now.

▲ What do you think this poem is about?

_____

▲ What title would you give this poem?

_____

▲ Now, fill in these facts about haikus.

A haiku has _____ lines.

The first line has _____ syllables.

The second line has _____ syllables.

The third line has _____ syllables.

A haiku has a total of _____ syllables.

SPELLING AND
PHONICS KS1

Haiku, see page 89

My haiku poem

My haiku poem is about

_____

These are some of the words that I may want to use in my poem:

_____   _____   _____

_____   _____   _____

_____   _____   _____

_____   _____   _____

▲ *Before you start writing*, remember that your haiku must be 3 lines long and it needs 5 syllables in the first line, 7 syllables in the second line and 5 syllables in the last line.

This is my haiku poem:

Line 1 _____

_____

Line 2 _____

_____

Line 3 _____

_____

My poem is called

_____

Introducing consonants and vowels, see page 94

Consonants and vowels

Name _____   Date _____

Here is the alphabet:

a b c d e f g h i j k l m n o p q r s t u v w x y z

▲ Look at the alphabet and draw a circle round the five vowels.

▲ Now write your name:

_____

▲ Draw a circle round all the vowels in your name.

How many vowels has your name got?

My name has _____ vowels.

How many consonants has your name got?

My name has _____ consonants.

Curriculum Bank
149

SPELLING AND
PHONICS KS1

Photocopiables

Letter string challenge, see page 101

Game record sheet

Name _____   Date _____

My letter string _____   Time allowed _____

Words containing my letter string

_____

_____

_____

_____

_____

_____

_____

_____

_____

_____

_____

_____

_____

I played with _____

I spelled _____ words correctly.

_____ was the winner!

SPELLING AND
PHONICS KS1

Letter string challenge, see page 101

Graphic knowledge assessment sheet

Name:	Age: Date:
Languages spoken:	

Comment on the child's ability to:

▲ recognise and name vowels. *(List vowels.)*	
▲ recognise and name consonants. *(List consonants.)*	
▲ recognise initial double consonant blends beginning with 's'. *(List blends.)*	
▲ recognise initial double consonant blends beginning with other letters. *(List blends.)*	
▲ spell common words using initial consonant blends. *(List words.)*	
▲ recognise common letter strings. *(List targeted letter strings.)*	
▲ spell words containing specified letter patterns. *(List targeted patterns and words.)*	

Other comments:

Attach '*Letter string challenge* game record sheet(s)' when played.

**SPELLING AND
PHONICS KS1**

Verb suffixes Pelmanism, see page 104

Verb roots (1)

post	start	add
end	plant	kick
work	show	bump
play	melt	allow
laugh	fill	listen
talk	open	shout

Verb suffixes Pelmanism, see page 104

Verb roots (2)

buy	pay	say
hear	send	eat
think	stand	break
fall	catch	grow
hold	drink	meet
speak	spend	tell

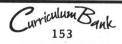

SPELLING AND
PHONICS KS1

Verb suffixes Pelmanism, see page 104

Verb suffixes

-ed	-ed	-ed
-ed	-ed	-ed
-ing	-ing	-ing
-ing	-ing	-ing
-ing	-ing	-ing
-ing	-ing	-ing

SPELLING AND
PHONICS KS1

Fixing opposites, see page 106

Words and prefixes

happy	sure	clean
certain	do	fair
hurt	dress	kind
lucky	selfish	tidy
well	appear	able
agree	obey	content
please	un	honest
afraid	button	dis

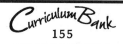

Fixing opposites, see page 106

Opposites record sheet (1)

Original word	Opposite	Meaning of opposite

SPELLING AND
PHONICS KS1

Fixing opposites, see page 106

Opposites record sheet (2)

Prefix: _____

Original word	New word with prefix

SPELLING AND PHONICS KS1

INFORMATION TECHNOLOGY WITHIN PHONICS & SPELLING AT KEY STAGE 1

The information technology activities outlined in this book can be used to develop and assess children's IT capability as outlined in the National Curriculum. Types of software rather than names of specific programs have been mentioned to enable teachers to use the ideas regardless of the computers used.

Main IT Focus

The main emphasis for the development of IT capability within these activities is on communicating information.

However, in this area of the curriculum there are many software packages which support children's learning in specific activities highlighted in this book. Teachers may still want to use specific software which operates on their computers and which addresses the content and understanding of the subject being taught. Although such software is not specifically mentioned within the text (much being only available for certain computers) some of the more useful of such software is mentioned later within this section. Many of the activities in this book are very practically based and give children opportunities to use concrete materials and resources to develop their understanding and use of language. Content specific software should not be used to replace such experiences but to develop or reinforce understanding only after initial practical work. Teachers should also be aware that although such software may assist pupils in developing language skills, it may add little to the development of their pupils' IT capability.

Word processors

During Key Stage 1 pupils will be developing their confidence and competence to use the standard computer keyboard. They should be taught a range of basic keyboard and word processing skills. These should include:

▲ an understanding of the layout of the keyboard and where the letter and number keys are found.

▲ how to get capital letters found above the number keys, using the *shift* key.

▲ how to use the delete key to erase words and letters.

▲ how to use the *cursor/arrow* keys, or mouse to position the cursor at the desired position.

▲ the use of more than a single finger/hand when typing, particularly as they become more proficient and know where letters are located.

▲ how to use the space bar; using their thumbs to press the space bar.

▲ how the word processor will 'wrap' the text around the end of the line so there is no need to press *return* at the end of each line.

▲ how to join text using the delete key.

▲ how to separate text or create new lines using the *return* key.

▲ how to move the cursor to a mistake and correct it, rather than deleting all the text back to the mistake, making the correction and then retyping the deleted text.

▲ how to print out their completed work, initially with support from the teacher, but eventually on their own.

Children will also need to save their work if they are unable to finish it in one session. They should be taught how to do this onto the hard or floppy disc so that eventually they can do it without teacher assistance. They will then need to be shown how to locate and retrieve their work at a later date.

Young children will take a long time to enter text at the keyboard so it is important to ensure that the writing tasks are kept short and that where possible there is other support available to teach and assist the child's development. If parents or other adults are available they can often be used in this way, provided they have the relevant skills, and know when to intervene. Alternatively they can be used for scribing for longer tasks, typing in the children's work and then going through it with them to edit and alter it.

For many of the writing tasks children can use the standard page format that is presented to them when the software is started. However for more complex tasks the teacher may wish to set up the page layout before the children start and save it, for example, as the menu layout. Children can then start with this basic menu layout and then begin to alter it if they need to.

Concept keyboards

Many school have access to concept keyboards which can be linked to the word processor through a user port, serial port or on later versions through the parallel port. Teachers should check which computer they are using to determine the type of connection needed. The keyboard itself is a grid of touch sensitive pads which when pressed pass a message to the computer. Two sizes of concept keyboards, A4 and A3, are in common use. Unfortunately although both have the same number of sensitive pads, the aspect ratio for these two keyboards is different and overlays prepared on one size cannot be enlarged or reduced using a photocopier to fit on another size. A more recent keyboard (Informatix) has a greater number of touch sensitive pads, is linked through the parallel port so that it can be used on most computers and can be used for a greater range of activities.

Concept keyboards can be used with great effect for children at the start of Key Stage 1 when language and writing skills, particularly the use of the keyboard, are at an early stage of development. The small pads of the concept keyboard can be programmed so that when a child presses the picture of a toothbrush the word will appear on the screen of the word processor. Other pads can be programmed to move the cursor around the screen, delete letters and then act as a RETURN key.